CW00917025

ETERNAL TRUTH
OF
THE SPIRIT WITHIN

Book One

written by
Barry Robinson
with help
gratefully
received
from
*Teachers in
The Spirit
World*

Blue Ocean Publishing

Eternal Truth of the Spirit Within: Book One

Published by Blue Ocean Publishing
St John's Innovation Centre
Cowley Road
Cambridge CB4 0WS
United Kingdom

www.blueoceanpublishing.biz

A catalogue record for this book is available from the British Library.
ISBN 978-1-907527-22-7

The Concise Oxford Dictionary, 10th Edition
Edited by Pearsall (2002)
Definition of '*truth*' by permission of Oxford University Press

For details of other books in this series and the companion audio collection please visit:
www.eternalspiritwithin.com

For Lilian

Carole, this book is for you.
To read. To cherish. To absorb. To find
your truth within yourself. To find
guidance to show you the way. To find
illumination and knowledge of the Spirit.
Please enjoy this book and don't rush.
Take your time reading it.

MY CHILD, KNOW THAT WE ARE WITH
YOU AND FEEL OUR LOVE ABOUT AND
IN YOU AS YOU LIVE YOUR LIFE
MAY PEACE, JOY AND LOVE BE
YOURS EVERMORE,
AMEN

Barry Olstein   7.3.16

Warning:

Please note that this book
is not intellectual in nature,
that is to say, its content makes no sense
for it contains *nothing*.

You contain everything
you need to know
and
you carry it
within your heart.

**You are a free Spirit
born of God
living within the eternal love
of Divine Presence**

THE CONTENTS OF BOOK ONE

Foreword
Introduction

PART I : THE START OF THIS BOOK
   1. Where Has This Book Come From Then?

PART II : THE BEGINNING OF THIS BOOK
   2. So What is it All About?
   3. The Purpose of This Book

PART III : ANOTHER BEGINNING OF THIS BOOK
   4. Peacefulness
   5. Life is Now
   6. The Big Funfair
   7. The Carousel
   8. Creation of the Carousel
   9. Be Still
  10. Fate and Free Will
  11. Cause and Effect
  12. Emotional Energy
  13. Resistance
  14. Responsibility
  15. Creativity
  16. A Game of Tennis
  17. A World of Thought
  18. A World of Nature
  19. The Nature of Fear
  20. Survival
  21. The Schoolroom
  22. The Playground
  23. Balance
  24. Reflection
  25. Light
  26. Integrity
  27. Evolution

PART IV : YET ANOTHER BEGINNING OF THIS BOOK
    28. Life Bursts Forth
    29. Joyful Growth
    30. Abundance
    31. Negative Expression
    32. Positive Expression
    33. Respectfulness
    34. Thoughtfulness
    35. Mindfulness
    36. The Silent Pool
    37. Meditation
    38. Inspiration
    39. Perception
    40. Visualisation
    41. In The Picture
    42. A Photograph
    43. Simplicity
    44. Protection
    45. Heal Thyself
    46. The Tug of War
    47. The Washing Machine
    48. Your Sense of Reality
    49. Etheric Body
    50. Sensitivity
    51. Awareness

PART V : THE END OF THIS BOOK
    52. A Walk in the Park
    53. I Believe

PART VI : CONTEMPLATIONS
    54. Some Thoughts to Contemplate
    55. The White Telephone
    56. The Castle of the Holy Grail
    57. God is Love
    58. To Know Love
    59. You Are
    60. To Find Love
    61. Feel The Spirit
    62. I Am That I Am
    63. I am, Within and Without

    Conclusion
    Afterword

Foreword

In God's House

Knock and the doorway shall be opened
wherein shall ye find truth shown to thee
and thou shalt know.

Amen

Introduction

Essentially, this book is about *remembering* and your life will change as a consequence of you reading it. If you are already conscious of walking your *path*, then you will know this already and some of the reasons why this happens are contained herein. There may not be much new here for you perhaps. It is, however, simply my purpose to help you to touch and feel once more that knowledge which is deep within your being. To bring to mind that which you *are*.

An old proverb says, 'it is wise to cross a river one stone at a time'. To best understand the contents of this book first read it through in order from the beginning to the end, in the same manner in which it has been written, one paragraph at a time and one page after the other. Thereafter you may choose, if you so wish, to dip into various subjects and pages at your leisure.

To get the most out of this book, I recommend strongly that you *do* read it in the order that it has been written. If you will study not just the words but also the spaces between the words, you may begin to see profound truths which are invisible to your everyday perception. In this way, so will you realise much more than these words are able to explain.

If you scrutinise this text with just your physical vision and your intellect, then you may find nothing but confusion within these pages. If you will use your second sight however, your sense of clairvoyance, then so shall you begin to understand the inner truth. It is necessary to use the inner vision to find inner meaning, to see that which is hidden from view.

The narrative has been written with a natural flow which has its own secret rhythms and sounds. This music, ethereal in nature, softly underlies the main musical themes of this book. To hear it, you will need to use your sense of clairaudience.

Read it in the same way that you listen to your favourite piece of music. As the sound falls upon your ears, so you hear the musical notes audibly in a physical sense. But you also hear the melodies with your *inner* ear. You feel the music within your heart and thus you perceive the message being given to you from the composer.

So find a quiet space.
Sit down and relax.
Be ready to listen.

**Allow the words on these pages to ring out loud
and clear in your ears**

PART I

THE START OF THIS BOOK

Where Has This Book Come From Then?

So here I am in the *big game* of my life, a championship league match to be sure. It must be so because, after a quiet start, it has most definitely been a pretty intense experience and at times I've found myself completely knackered. Far too much exertion and running around in circles. I must be well into the second half by now, but since I have been so preoccupied with it all I don't really have a clue as to what time the Big Clock is showing. When that final whistle eventually blows however I won't much care, because the relief will be enormous. I shall refresh myself after the match and then go off for a good night out on the town.

The last time I remember any serious clock watching was when I was third mate out at sea somewhere and I was absolutely whacked. For the life of me, I simply cannot remember the reasons why. I was so tired, in fact, that I could barely stay awake! It was the longest four hours I've ever been through and the last hour of that watch was the longest 60 minutes that I have ever experienced. In this particular lifetime and possibly all my other lifetimes as well. I shall check up on this point when I get back properly later.

In order to stay awake, every few minutes I had to stick my head out over the front of the bridge wing to receive a blast of cold air travelling upward at speeds of 30-40 knots or more. My God, I swear that clock stood still and did not move! At last, noon arrived and I got busy with the bridge routine. I was so relieved to finally get to my cabin and *turn in*. Now there's an old sailor term from the days of sail. It's so sad that the old nautical language seems to be dying out in Britain these days. As soon as my head hit that pillow my light went out. Bliss!

So back to the present moment then. Well, maybe. I can't say that I have lived a very religious or spiritual life this time around, but I am aware that I have done so previously. I was certainly a Christian monk a few centuries ago and I have been a Buddhist monk at least once. I don't remember whether I have been a Muslim cleric, but I am aware that I was once the young wife of an older merchant somewhere in Arabia. He was a wealthy man and I wore fine clothes and loved living by the sea. I had to go inland however, against my wishes, on a trading trip with him. I fell ill with a fever and died.

I am aware of many lives, including being an American airman during the last war. Some unhappy memories there! But I think my love of blues is from this time and I mean the real blues and not the pop music stuff. Sung by people who lived hard lives in hard times. My God, how they make those instruments talk! They sing and play from the depths of their souls. In my opinion, few modern musicians come anywhere near close to matching them.

I have also worked my way up through the ranks as a Roman soldier and lived as a tax collector in Hispania. I am not sure whether I retired from the army to the position or not. As I write these words, however, *I am* aware that the tax collector came from a privileged wealthy family and so this does seem to suggest a separate lifetime.

At school, I was very interested in all things Roman and even dreamt of building and living in a Roman Villa. If I ever get the money together I might still fulfil that dream, even if it is one from the past. Isn't it interesting how role playing has become such a popular pastime?

I've seen many people at weekends dressed up as Romans, Vikings, Medieval, Tudor, Renaissance, Victorians, Edwardians, English and American Civil War combatants. Even Second World War and the Fifties and Sixties. Absolutely fascinating, isn't it!

People agree to disagree over the subject of reincarnation. I think many would be surprised to find that it was once included within the teachings of the Early Christian Church. I do remember coming across the idea, however, that it was removed because the subject can be very open to speculation and distortion. For myself I think that we live just the one life, an eternal one. Our lifetimes are like the chapters of a book and each one is completely distinct in itself, yet somehow they are all linked and bound together. They are all closely interconnected as *one*.

We may remember things sometimes if it is useful to a situation. I was always asking about why I was feeling what I was feeling emotionally, since it didn't seem to be very relevant to my life at the time. As information began to come forward about my previous time here as the airman, I kept on asking for more. One day, I was talking directly to a good friend of mine during a trance session. A guide, he told me that I was meant to forget about it all and that I had. He told me that I was like a dog with a bone who wouldn't let go. He told me that I should let old bones stay in the ground.

I realised later on that we need to forget for a very good reason. We all have enough on our plates already and it is not wise to overburden ourselves. So it really is best then to forget, as the information is not required for the time being. There is definitely much more to this earthly existence than most of us ever realise.

I feel sure that much of the time life is enjoyable, so it is best to forget the uncomfortable periods. As my wonderful friend said, *it is best to let old bones stay in the ground*. As regards this lifetime, I don't really have much recall of my early life. It just seemed to happen smoothly with nothing much to worry me. Life must have been good then. I can remember certain moments in particular, which seem to stand out for some reason. I call them *psychic* memories because I can relive the moment complete with a sense of the atmosphere, the smells and the textures. Perhaps you have also experienced something similar.

Born in West London, I was nine years old when the family moved to Cambridge. My physical life, in a certain sense, didn't really start properly until after the 11+ exam when the big outside world rudely began to interfere with my nice calm quiet existence. I can remember very clearly sitting in the classroom at my new school, feeling a bit dismayed that I was going to be there for the next five years. So I decided there and then, that I just had to join in with *the game*. Otherwise it wasn't going to be a very useful time at all.

Unexpectedly, I found myself at the top of the class. It was puzzling because all I was doing was paying attention in the classroom and then just writing it all up for homework that night. Things went reasonably well although I can't say that I was really very happy with all of this. Then one day something deep and profound happened. It was during the third year, in a chemistry or physics lesson and something was said to the class.

I cannot remember the remark made by the teacher but the response I experienced within me was so overpowering that it was to change my life. It felt as if my whole being seemed to shout out loud all at once....   *No, that statement is just not true!*

From that intense moment onwards, I found that I couldn't fully engage in *the game* any more. I seemed to lose my joy and life started to become hard work, it all became a bit of a struggle.

That day, my *inner truth* had shouted out loud to me and it was impossible to ignore it. Slowly, I became aware that I was observing myself as I lived my life. The tension between the two perspectives heightened considerably and I was not happy at all. I continuously felt some sort of indescribable angst deep within me, which just would not go away. I began to question things. I began to live an inner and an outer life.

Finally, I sat down to write.
To write a book about my truth.
It has been calling out to me now
for 45 years, ever since that fateful day
at school.

And so here it is....

PART II

THE BEGINNING OF THIS BOOK

So What is it All About?

Maybe you are one of the lucky souls, whose life is good and fun.
Everything just seems to fall into place easily and at the right time.
If so, that's fine. Just great. You are doing very well indeed.
Please do carry on and live your life to the full.

But maybe you struggle sometimes to make sense of this world.
Have you ever felt bewildered or confused?
Are you occasionally puzzled or frustrated about things?
Are you unable to feel as good about life as you might wish?
Do unfortunate circumstances sometimes happen around you?

Have you ever asked the question, *Why?*
If so, then perhaps this book may be just right for you.

An answer given to this big question is famously 42.
This might be a correct answer, believe it or not!
'How so?' you may say.
'That doesn't seem to make any sense whatsoever!'

Oh, yes it does!
I suggest you have a look at the subject of numerology.
$$42 \text{ is then.... } 4 + 2 = 6$$
The 6 is an interesting number which when inverted
becomes a 9, the *Cosmic Number*.
So do you understand yet?

It has often been written that numbers
contain all the secrets of the Universe.
Maybe that is a truth.

Consider *Isaac Newton* and his *Laws*, upon which modern
engineering has been built.
Consider *Theoretical Physics*, which has put men upon the moon
and built quantum computers.

All is based upon the simple and logical use of numbers.
Now do you understand yet?
No? Oh Dear!

Imagine yourself holding a piece of wood.
It is 3 feet, or about a metre, in length.
Your hand is in the middle.
Feel the texture of that wood.
Smell the fragrance of that wood.
Feel the shape and the weight of that wood.
Now hold it out horizontally in front of you.

You look at it and see that there is an end to the Left.
And also an end to the Right.
So the length of wood that you are holding has two ends.
A Left and a Right.
'Nothing complicated here!' you may say.

In your imagination, now spin the piece of wood
through 180 Degrees.
At first sight, it seems that nothing has changed.
And on the face of it, this is true.
You are still holding the piece of wood in the middle.
And there are still ends to the Left and to the Right.
'Yes, that's simple to understand!' you may say.

However, the Left end is now the Right end and *vice versa*.
So yes, we can say that the piece of wood has two opposite ends.
Yet although opposite, they seem also to be interchangeable.
Everything has stayed the same and yet everything has changed.

In the *Physical Sense* there are no opposites, only Relative Position.

In the same way, love and hate seem to be opposites and yet both are interchangeable. At some time or other, you may have seen or heard these words.... *I loved you once but now I hate you*.

In the *Emotional Sense* there are no opposites, only Relative Values.

Philosophy might state that if there are no opposites, then so must *All be One*.

In the *Intellectual Sense* there are no differences, only Unity.

We now all live in a world where everyone is more connected than ever before known. Communication can now be instant, almost anywhere in the world, provided that you are linked to a signal.

In the *Psychic Sense* there is no separation, only Connection.

Spiritual Teaching, that is to say, teachings from the spirit within says that *All is Love*.

In the *Spiritual Sense* there is only Love.

But what exactly is this Love?

Well, that is the question I once asked God many years ago.
It was a question to which I received an immediate answer, in a
most unexpected way.

So this book then, is my attempt to pass on to you some of the
answers to the many questions I have asked of God over the years,
as I tried to make sense of this perplexing life all around me.

If you have no questions and enjoy a perfect understanding of
yourself and the world, then you may have little need perhaps to
read this book.
I wish you all the best, I really do.
With all the love in this world and the next.

But if not and everything still
looks to be as clear as mud to you,
then please do read on.

> *I ask only for you to keep an open mind*
> *and that you are ready for the challenges ahead.*

May truth
softly touch your heart
and
you recognise its gentle caress

The Purpose of This Book

The purpose of this book is to help you to find and understand

Truth.

Your Truth.

Your Own Truth.

Not the Truth of Anyone Else.

Because Truth Belongs to You Alone.

It has absolutely nothing to do with anyone else.
And yet paradoxically it includes everyone else.
Herein lies a Conundrum.
And it's a Big One.

How on Earth can we make any sense of it when, on the face of it, it truly does seem to make no sense at all. It's all a nonsense really. We look at something and see one thing, then look deeper and see something different. How do we determine which aspect is more true than the other? If we say that both are equally true, how do we then determine the greater truths from the minor ones?

In fact,
how do we ever find
the truth
the *whole* truth
and nothing but the truth.

The Concise Oxford Dictionary, 10th Edition, Completely Revised, Page 1540:

Truth n. (pl. truths)	the quality or state of being true
(also **the truth**)	that which is true as opposed to false
	a fact or belief that is accepted as true

Phrases:
in truth   really, in fact
to tell the truth
truth to tell
if truth be told   to be frank

Origin Old English:
triewth, treowth   *faithfulness, constancy*

I have personally found words and the meanings of words to be a wonderful source of knowledge and inspiration.

Is it not a most marvellous thing? To see how humans have developed not just the one but many languages to express their thoughts. At first verbally and then latterly in written form.
So if we ponder, that is to say, weigh the meaning of this word *truth* what do we find?

Perhaps we find that a truth is a fact.
An accepted fact.
A belief that a fact is true.
Well, frankly yes, that is the case.

The Concise Oxford Dictionary, 10th Edition, Completely Revised,
Page 508:

Fact n. (pl. facts)   a thing that is indisputably the case

Origin 15th Century: original meaning *an act*, later *a crime*
                          surviving in the phrase,
                          before (or after) the fact

        from the Latin *factum*, and the verb *facere*, to do

A fact then is something which is *done*.
So it turns out not to be solid and real at all.
It is not the concrete reality of things surrounding us,
as we might at first have thought.
Or is it?

Perhaps a building is a fact after the fact of building the building.
Thus a fact is, in fact, an action.
The act of doing something.
An event which happens.
Now that is a real surprise, is it not?

Well, it has certainly surprised me!
And that's a fact.
Impressed?
I am, words never fail me.
I am never lost for words.
My friends can confirm that, as a fact.

Ah!
But what about the idea that something has a *quality* of truth.
Is this not subjective analysis?
A concept and not a fact?
OMG!

At first sight, *truth* seems to be such a simple thing.
Yet the more we look at it, the less straightforward it appears to be.
Oh, dear!

I have often found that studying the original meanings and sources
of the words we use most illuminating.

So let us look again at the definition and its origins.
We find that the word contains the sense of *faithfulness* and
the sense of *constancy*.

What do these concepts mean for you?
To me they suggest trust and dependability.
The truth is something which we can rely upon.
The truth is something we can put our faith upon.

To find truth we need to trust

PART III

ANOTHER BEGINNING OF THIS BOOK

Peacefulness

"It is time, my friend. Let us begin our work. Let us take the time to relax and blend together, so that our words may flow easily to you and onto the page in front of you. For we have a great work to accomplish and we need your help to achieve this goal. Feel at ease as we begin to work with you. All is well.

At last you have stopped. You have let go. Become still. At last you have found out who you are. Your talent. You are a writer and you came to write. To put thoughts and ideas down onto paper.

To pass those thoughts on to others who cannot access the information directly. Your skill is to connect to the world of thoughts and we can make use of this talent, in order that we may pass our thoughts to others who are ready to receive our wisdom and knowledge."

Peace. To be still. To feel relaxed and at one with both yourself and the world around you. When we feel calmness within then can we easily reach for our joy, which also lies deep within. But how can we achieve this ideal?

The truth is that when we focus upon things and events in the world which make us feel uneasy, then so also do we become uneasy within ourselves. It is as if we reflect, within our feelings, that which we give our attention to from the world around us.

And so eventually do we feel unease. Do we feel a lack of peace. If we continue to look at upsetting realities in this Universe, so do we begin to feel stress and then finally, distress. Illness and disease follow.

All this we experience because somehow we have allowed our attention to wander away from pleasant realities, towards that which does not make us feel good. It is our reactions to life then which causes us to lose our peacefulness.

So to think peaceful thoughts will help us to create a calm and peaceful presence of mind within. Help us to be still. And in this way can we reduce and eventually cease that feeling of stress and dis-ease, which we all experience at some time during our lives.

So our message ultimately is a message of peace. We would wish to see more peace in this world. For when we can feel *peace*, then so also are we more able to fully experience *love*. And when we can achieve a deeper knowing of love, so then can we truly feel our *joy*.

A joy so deep and fulfilling, so strong and exhilarating that our hearts will feel full to bursting point. And the more joy that we can feel, then the more *alive* we can become in every sense of the word. More vitality, more energy and more well-being.

So our message to the world is a message of peace. And we know that with this peace will come more love. And with this love will come more joy. Thus we wish for you, my friend and for *all* the world....   more peace, love and joy.

May peace be thine

Life is Now

How then can we fulfil our dream? By attempting to give to you a deeper understanding of both yourself and of the life that you live. You chose of your own free will to be born into a physical body, in order that you could experience more fully this sense of being *alive*.

You came to experience life in all its forms. Its ups and downs. Its lefts and rights. Its dreams and despairs. You came to feel all these wonderful sensations of *being* and *living* within this physical environment of Earth and you came to enjoy it!

———————————————

Sooner or later, we all die and we thus will let go of the physical body. When we do so we will take with us all of our experiences back to another world. That world wherein we all truly abide and have our being.

The world from which we are communicating in this very moment, *now*. No matter who or where you are, in this life or the afterlife, your life is now. It *is*, in this moment. It *is*, eternally now.

As they say, life goes on. And we wish to assure you most sincerely should you still have any doubts about this matter, that indeed it does. Deep within your being, you know this to be so.

Therefore, we ask for you to relax and worry not that you will run out of time. We might say perhaps, that time itself does not exist. There is only this moment, *now*. Life is about living, *now*. Being in this moment, *now*. So please do try to enjoy this moment as much as possible.

For the time being, while you are focusing upon living this physical experience, do try to have some fun. Do not dwell over-much upon small details which may cause some upset now and then. Which may cause you to experience stress. Which may cause you to experience the lack of peaceful thoughts.

If you can, try not to let anyone or anything disturb your sense of inner peacefulness. We know that it is not easy to feel at ease when something has caused you to feel unease. If this be so, then try to find for yourself something more enjoyable to think about instead.

Go for a walk. Have a sleep. Listen to the silence. Listen to music. Sit in a chair and become as still as possible. Talk to your pet if you have one. Talk to the wildlife around you, if not.

Move your attention away from the source of your unease. Try to change your focus to something which makes you *feel good*. And so eventually will you then begin to feel the return once more of your ease.

You may wonder perhaps, why we would suggest that you talk to your pets or the wildlife which lives about you. It is because they are content with life and go with the flow. It is because they live in the moment. It is because they feel at ease with themselves and with the world around them.

So be easy about your life and try not to give yourself a hard time. If you can, let go of your worries and relax a little. Try to live your life for this moment. *Now!*

Relax and enjoy your life

The Big Funfair

Roll up, Roll up, All the Fun of the Fair,
All the Rides are Free,
If You Dare,
All the Fun of the Fair!

Imagine yourself, if you will, sitting upon a white cloud somewhere in heaven. All is well with the *Universe, Creation* and *All That Is*. Peace and love surround you. You are in a state of pure bliss. You are in a state of ecstasy. You *are*. You are the *is* in the *All That Is*.

Suddenly, you hear a faint sound. It is so faint, in fact, that you decide it is your imagination playing tricks on you. But the sound seems to persist. Unconsciously, it has gradually become louder and louder until you are able to discern different sounds within the sound. In truth, you are feeling the sound rather than listening to it.

You realise that you are feeling the vibrational energy of those sounds. The state of pure bliss and ecstasy is just a faint memory now. Suddenly, you are *aware* of colours swirling within the energy field of this sound. The edge of your vision has now become a grey mist as you are drawn more and more into the beautiful and radiant vibrant waves of indescribably iridescent colours of the *Light*.

Colour and Sound merge together, as one. You have become the *colour*. You have become the *sound*. You notice now that you have yourself become a *being* of colour and sound. It is the most wonderful experience that you have ever remembered!

As the sound and colour begin to gradually take shape, so do you also. It feels so good. The sound begins to take shape into voices. The colour begins to take shape into form. You start to discern voices and you recognise them. You start to feel yourself take form and it feels familiar and comfortable to you.

You are aware of beings around you. You feel their love and affection for you. It feels so good to be back amongst everyone. You feel activity and movement. There are things to do. Places to be. Just like the old times, you remember.

A group of friends whom you know extremely well is gathered about you and memories are shared and good times are re-lived. There is much laughter and joy. It is so good to feel this close companionship again. It feels great to be back within the family group and to feel such beautiful warmth of love once more.

Together as one, you all seem to shout the same collective thought, *Let's Go Then!* And so you do. You sense movement and now become aware that you are standing in a *Great Concourse* where a multitude of souls are milling around, all busy doing something. At first you all pull together, in shock, as you suddenly feel everything that is going on. But adapting very quickly, you all begin to relax and the new situation does seem to be vaguely familiar somehow.

As you all take stock of your new surroundings, a very imposing figure materialises amongst you and announces that he is to be your *Group Administrator* for the trip. He has with him tickets which have been organised beforehand and proceeds to give them out to everyone. He is definitely a familiar face but somehow none of you can quite remember who he is.

Someone spots a Steward holding up a sign with all your names upon it. She comes over, smiles broadly and you all hear the words *follow me!* And so you do. The hustle and bustle is getting much more intense now and you all huddle together more tightly as you move deeper into the crowds. The Guide leads everyone to a huge gateway. Over the top can be seen an enormous illuminated sign. It is calling out loud in musical tones, *Welcome To Earth - The Greatest Funfair in This Part of the Galaxy.* And so in you all go.

You approach a line of smaller gates now and the signs above them are in different languages, some seem familiar and others are not. More Guides have appeared and various people go off elsewhere. Your little group has now gathered before a particular gate and you all hear the sound of the voices calling out to you....

Roll up, Roll up, All the Fun of the Fair,
All the Rides are Free,
If You Dare,
All the Fun of the Fair!

You hand in your tickets to the attendant on duty and in you all go. It's absolutely incredible! As far as the eye can see are fairground rides of every description and in between are seen countless stalls offering games and wares of every kind. The noise inside is almost deafening as the stall vendors and ride organisers call out to attract customers. With all the bright flashing lights and loud music, it is very bewildering at first until you learn to adapt and re-adjust your focus.

The Group splits up into smaller parties which go off in different directions. Some head towards the *Big Wheel* for the views. Some go for the *Rides of Fear* or the *Rides of Speed* and one heads off towards the *Ghost Train*. You decide to visit a *Refreshment Area* with a few close friends, to use up some promotional vouchers which came with your ticket. Mmmm, that food smells so good!

You are approaching a *Tea Stand* when you are all stopped by two security guards who start talking to one of the young lads. An argument follows and it turns out that he only has a *Day Ticket* and must leave the Funfair immediately. He's been in a few hours now and is totally mesmerised by it all. But the guards are very strict and inform him that he has to go. They recommend that he tries to get a *Full Pass* the next time around if he wants to come back.

Everyone is having a great time, but suddenly one of the party disappears into a *Bar Tent*. He is holding in his hand special offers which a salesman has just given to him and he is not seen again.

After an enjoyable trip into a sideshow, you are all wondering what to do next when a great shout goes up. There has been an accident and someone has fallen off one of the *Motorcycle Rides*. Sadly, you all realise that the victim was someone you knew well.

The mood within the group has become more sombre now but still there is great enjoyment to be had. With enthusiasm you all head off towards the *Dodgems* but while you are making your way there another great shout goes up. A *Roller-Coaster* nearby has collapsed and many have been injured or killed.

As you are all walking along the Avenue, a dark wave of heavy sorrow washes over everyone. Two of the group are overwhelmed with such sadness that they just cannot go on and sit down on a bench. One member of the party has worked in the big *Hospital Tent* before on a previous visit to the fair. She declares that she will go there to lend a hand.

It's time for some fun! Depleted in number, the group moves off to find the *Dodgems*. It's great entertainment and also very exciting too! Some hooligan has damaged a machine and is now driving it about madly, causing mayhem. Suddenly with a loud bang four machines crash together. Attendants rush forward to help and find that three people have been seriously injured. They are carried off to the *Hospital Tent*.

You all decide to leave the *Ride* and to steer clear of rogue drivers in the future. Your very best friend tells you that you seem to have put on a lot of weight and you begin to regret using up all of those food vouchers. After all, they were only an option and had not been compulsory.

The idea is put forward to go and find a *Spa Tent* for some serious body pampering. Whilst there, you find that you have become very interested in the therapies and so you make some arrangements to visit them again on a future trip to the Fair. You leave the *Spa Tent*, very impressed that your health is now back to normal.

But to get back onto the main thoroughfare everyone has to walk through a dark, dimly lit area. People are staring at your small band with furtive eyes. Suddenly a shadow rushes out and one of the party is mugged. You all pull together for protection. But one of your friends is so affected by this dramatic event that she goes off to become a security guard.

Many years have now passed and the group split up long ago, with people going their own way. You spend all of your time now with your very best friend. You go everywhere together.

Life experience has taught you to be wary of some stall vendors who are deceitful and to stay away from certain *Rides* which are not maintained well and so therefore are in a dangerous and unsafe condition. Spending your time together in more quiet pastimes now, you tend to gravitate towards the parks and more peaceful spaces.

No longer feeling a need for excitement and thrills, life has taught you to stay away from the shadowy places and the shady dealers, thieves and pickpockets who inhabit them. You choose to stay in the more open and light areas now and you are happy to let them live, as they so wish, within the darker shadows of the Fairground.

Life is much more tranquil now. But all those negative experiences over the years have gradually taken their toll on the health of both of you. Sadly, your very best friend has fallen ill and has had to leave the Fairground.

Eventually, you too find that your *Pass* has expired and the security guards come to take you back to the gateway. After filling in the necessary paperwork, you meet up once more with your Guide who greets you most warmly. You are full of all the experiences that you have just had and there is so much to talk about.

Together you both walk out onto the *Great Concourse* and you see your very best friend, waiting there for you. You are so elated! With great joy you all go off to a Coffee House for some light refreshment and to catch up with each other.

You are having a grand time. A group of friends whom you know extremely well is gathered about you and memories are shared and good times are re-lived. There is much laughter and joy.

It is so good to feel this close companionship again. It feels great to be back within the family group and to feel such beautiful warmth of love once more.

You feel their love and affection for you. It feels good to be back amongst everyone. You feel activity and movement. There are things to do. Places to be. Just like the old times, *you remember*.

Trust that the purpose of your life is to have fun

The Carousel

Roll up. Roll up. All the fun of the fair. So my friend, what then is the purpose of it all? Is it just like a carousel? An endless-merry-go-round-of-existence in a celestial fairground? Are we all here just for the ride? Round and round?

And if we are all going round in perpetual circles then do we ever actually get anywhere? If existence has no beginning and no end, how then can it ever have any direction? If existence just exists, how then can it have any purpose or reason for being? Is it all just for the *fun* of the fair? No, surely not!

Is it the purpose to ask endless questions, questions and yet more questions? Yes. Perhaps it is, my friend, but only because to receive an answer is so rewarding and enjoyable. It's fun!

And the faster you ask the questions, the faster do you receive and thus experience the answers. Your head will spin dizzily and your life will swirl about you in-ever-decreasing-circles. Yes, maybe life is just like the merry-go-round-at-the-fair, an experience to savour and enjoy to the full.

Is it the purpose to enjoy action, activity and the pursuit of a goal? Yes. Perhaps it is, my friend, but only because to achieve a goal lends a value to the action. Value is an abstract notion, which itself is given substance through the action of doing something and there can be much satisfaction in the attainment of a goal.

If we continuously move on from one thing to the next, from one fairground attraction to another, do we not feel the need sometimes for a break? Do we not get tired? Do we not need relaxation?

The constant movement up and down, left and right, round and round can of itself become disorientating and confusing to the senses. Occasionally, do we not feel the need for some peace and quiet? A need to rest? A time to allow the physical body to recover its equilibrium and the mind to recover its balance?

To every action is a re-action. To every question is there an answer. When we ask question after question continuously, so then can the answers sometimes come back in a muddled confusion.

We cannot see the wood for the trees or is it the trees for the wood? We seem to be going round in circles. We become dizzy and lose our balance. We have a need to stand still.

It is as if sometimes that we feel the need to get off the wooden horse on the carousel. To stand upon the moving platform instead and then to begin to move inward towards the centre, where the motion is less. And if we are able to stand at the very centre of the merry-go-round then we find no movement at all, but instead do we find *stillness*.

Like the piece of wood with two opposite ends, the carousel has both motion and non-motion. It has movement yet is motionless at its centre. And so do we live a life full of action and movement yet always do we have stillness, deep within our being.

And a merry-go-round is created for the purpose of having fun, is it not? So maybe the purpose of life is, after all, to experience joy. So try if you can to relax. And be calm, be peaceful, be still. And at the same time, enjoy the ride....

Be calm as you go about your life

Creation of the Carousel

Whence comes this carousel? Does it appear as if by magic, from out of the very ether itself? The answer might surprise you, my friend. Because truly does it come into being as if from nowhere by magic. From nowhere to now here. It is as if the whole magnificent structure comes from nothing and so to understand the miracle of creation, must we try to understand nothing.

We would submit to you that to understand nothing, so then must you try to clear your mind of everything. All that you have ever learnt, every last thing. And if you are successful in this endeavour, what you shall be left with will be.... *nothing*.

But how shall I recognise that I have achieved this incredible feat? You must ask of yourself, the following question.... *of what do I now remember?* And the answer should be.... *nothing!*

So, my friend, what do you make of all this? Are you able, in fact, to make something of it? Maybe you make *nothing* from it? Have you been able to perceive the hidden secrets of creation yet? No? Oh dear! Then perhaps we should continue with our dissertation.

To create something out of nothing must be magical you say and you would be right. It is pure magic. The Latin word *magicus* is said to relate to a Greek word which means magus. The magus being a priest from ancient Persia. A wise man.

To create something out of nothing is hard to imagine, is it not? And to imagine something is to form an image of that something. So then to create anything must we first imagine it to be. Must we form an image of what is to be. And to form an image of something then must we first have some idea of what it is we wish to be.

We wish for you to read that last sentence again, as it might be very important for you. You may need to think about this, my friend. Perhaps we could say that we need to have an *idea* of something before we can create that something. Perhaps we could say then that our thought is the power of our creation.

With our thoughts do we not make our world? Maybe we should be more thoughtful of that which we think about in future. But whence comes our thought? Does it not seemingly appear to come from out of the thin air? Seem to come from nowhere? From *nothing?*

We wish for you to be still a moment and to look about you. What do you see? Are you within a building perhaps? If so, is not all that you see the product of someone's thought? You are surrounded by thought forms, *ideas* which have become into form. Remember, that everything first has started life as a thought.

But what if you are outside? In a garden, a park or a wood. On a beach by the sea or on the top of a high mountain. What do you see, but *God's Creation* before you? Whence then comes the idea or the thought of a tree, a rock, a river or a cloud? The Universe about us is created by thought. Now that truly is *a big idea*, is it not?

We have been playing with words and the meanings of words, much to our great delight and we hope for your enjoyment also. But what *are* these words exactly? We would say that they are the creation of our thoughts, the expression of our thoughts. They are our ideas made into form, made real in this world. Our ideas made a reality. Our ideas being realised.

In the beginning was God, and the word was thought

Be Still

Godly, I know that I am. But if you are God, then who *are* you? Are you an old man with a long white beard and possibly long white hair also, sitting upon a great golden throne somewhere? We most certainly hope not! We would suggest that if indeed this is the case, then that must be a consequence of your imagination and not ours.

It is said that God is omnipotent and omnipresent. But you may say that you feel limited. That you feel small and insignificant. And if this is so, how then can you possibly be God?

'Look at the enormous size of the Universe!' you say. 'How can you say that I am God?' you say. We would say, however, that the truth is as always very simple. So much so that it cannot be easily seen or perceived.

You are a thinker. You think therefore you *are*. And with your thoughts you create. You are a creator, made in the image of God. And if you are made in an image of God, then of necessity must you be also the thought of God. You are *being* the thought of God. You are a *being* of God. And so therefore art thou not of, by and from God itself?

You are a thinker. You think therefore you *are*. Your thoughts will become actions and events, facts. Thus you live the consequence of those thoughts. Does not your life somehow just seem to happen?

Action is an expression of energy, is it not? Thus you also must be an expression of energy. Motion and emotion. Energy in motion and thought in motion. Einstein declared that light is an expression of energy. If you are energy then it follows also that you are light.

At last, we have here some *illumination*. We can now cast some light upon the matter in question. Matter which was first a thought. Thought which becomes form and form which becomes matter. So, if that matter is connected to light and *light* is the illumination of our thoughts then so must it be also that you are God, by default.

Did you follow all that? Did you manage to connect everything together there? Perhaps your mind is racing and spinning around, like a carousel. If so, get off the horse and take a break. Be still for the moment. Be still and *know*. Stand at the centre of your thoughts and observe what *is*.

If God is *All That Is* and you are connected to God, so must you also be of God. And since *all* connects with the same energy, so must you also be of God. And since *all* is the being of this energy, so must you also be of God.

We could say that *all* thought is God-given. As you are essentially a product of your thoughts, then so must you also be a product of the thought of God. And thus a part of the being of God and yet also apart of the being of God. It is as if we are a part of and yet also apart from the nature of God.

Like the piece of wood with two ends and the carousel with motion and non-motion, we can be both a part of creation and yet also apart from creation. We are able both to experience it and to observe it. Although we may often feel alone, yet are we never truly apart from God. For God *is* everything that exists. We are *all* God.

May the peace and the love and the joy of God be with you

Fate and Free Will

So, my friend, truly can we say that you are a most profound and godly individual. And that might seem perhaps to be quite a heavy responsibility for a mere human being. As a creator, we have the free will to be or do anything that we may wish to be or do. And as a result we create consequence. That which we have created then becomes our fate, that is to say, it then happens to us.

Imagine, if you will, someone who lives their whole life crossing roads without first looking out for traffic or other hazards. Perhaps they could manage to live to a good age and not come to any harm. But as we all know, of course, this is highly unlikely to be the case. So what is it exactly that determines their fate?

What is it that determines whether that person is injured or remains safe and healthy? And it would need to be a very determined individual indeed to live such a life. Perhaps it might be of help to us instead, to consider two very different groups of human beings.

One group will stay in good health and be long lived whilst the other perhaps, does not. We shall discuss the former group later on in the book but for the moment, let us now think about the latter.

Perhaps these people have been told as children that it is very dangerous to cross a road and that they must watch out for danger at all times. To listen and look, before ever crossing any road. It has been impressed upon them that they must be ever vigilant and wary whenever they decide to cross over any roadway.

Thus is an expectation created within their mind of danger and also perhaps, of fear. They have been told about accidents which have happened to other people. They see incidents on television and read about them in the newspapers. They even listen to the traffic news on their car radios as they drive along the highway.

And so finally do they actually *see* an accident involving other people before their very own eyes. And as a direct consequence of this experience, they begin to worry. They begin to think that something might also happen to them. The vision stays with them.

They then begin to imagine accidents which might befall them and they may even dream about it. However, they are mostly happy and confident as they go about their lives and these thoughts are not really very significant. But suddenly they experience a near miss.

Perhaps they are crossing a road on foot and a car nearly hits them. Or maybe they narrowly avoid an accident whilst driving their car. They are shocked. 'It came out of the blue!' they say. 'It appeared out of nowhere!' they say. ' That was unexpected!' they say. 'I didn't see that coming!' they say.

But yes, they did! For they saw it coming long before it happened to happen. They saw it in their mind's eye. For they have imagined it to be and they have thought about it. Remember my friend, that we are all creators. When we hold an image within our mind, then as a consequence that image may come into being and thus may be caused to be.

Truly then, are we made in the image of God. But fear not! Learn to take your life one step at a time, in much the same way as you once learned to walk as a tiny baby. Remain calm and keep your balance. You did not worry then and so why worry now?

Think peaceful thoughts and stay happy and in consequence shall your life be both happy and peaceful.

We stride forward with free will and cause our fate to follow in our footsteps

Cause and Effect

So we are made in the image of God. And we now understand more fully how we as creators can manifest our world, through the power of our thoughts. Now that is quite a responsibility, you might think. And you would be right. But fear ye not. For God does look after us with love and we always have what we need, although sometimes not always that which we might want.

To every thought is a consequence. Is this not an example of cause and effect? To every action is a reaction. Scientists and also many spiritual teachers too would call this observation a law. They might say that it is one of the most fundamental laws of the universe.

Gravity is an example of cause and effect in action and it affects *all* matter. In fact, there is nothing physical unaffected by this law. We can say then that it is truly universal in nature.

Strange is it not, how the most important things in life are taken for granted and just accepted without question. Like the air we breathe. Human life both begins and ends with a single breath, yet rarely do we give it much thought.

Similarly, the planets and stars are all moving due to the law of cause and effect yet we live upon this Earth blissfully unaware of everything which is happening around us. And if this planet was not being held within the equilibrium of the Solar System, then perhaps life as we know it could not exist.

This law then is absolutely essential to all life everywhere in the Universe. *To every action is a reaction*. And so in your life do you react to events, not just physically but also with your thoughts and emotions and in the same way as the moon moves the oceans so is created the ebb and flow of events within your life.

Consider, if you will, a vessel far out at sea steaming towards a destination. If the ship holds a steady bearing then will it make the desired landfall. However the wind and swell, the ocean currents and the compass error will all affect the ship's progress.

Leeway causes deviation over the ground from the course, even though the ship's wheel is held steady and true upon the desired heading. Sometimes the effects can be beneficial, assisting the vessel on her voyage and at other times can impede progress.

The Captain therefore must remain ever vigilant. Reacting always to events, he must constantly adjust the heading to compensate for leeway and loss of position. No matter what happens, the ship still steers for port and eventually arrives safe and sound. The pilot is picked up and the vessel proceeds to berth alongside.

In the same way do we live our lives. To achieve a goal so must we hold true to our vision, no matter what storms may befall us and no matter what temptations we may find in ports of call along the way.

If we are steadfast in our will, eventually shall we see the bright and welcoming beams of the lighthouse to guide us through the dangers of the shallows. The *light* shows us the way forward, until finally we safely make port.

The law of cause and effect is a constant. It is a *given* reality within which we all live. We might say it is a gift from God. We might say that it is like the great ocean upon which we steer our ship of life. It supports us at all times. It is always there for us. It never lets us down, come rain or shine.

May we trust in the everlasting love of God

Emotional Energy

Come rain or shine, we sail our ship of life across the surface of the great oceans of existence and the weather which we can so often experience could be said to be emotional in nature. Boldly do we steam ahead through the waves of cause and effect. And so we feel good in periods of fair weather and maybe not so good in the rough seas of bad weather.

Sometimes, we have to steer our way through the storms and heavy seas of emotional turmoil. We must remain vigilant as we stand our watch and change the autopilot to manual steering. Putting our hands upon the wheel we should steer into the big seas and try to anticipate the movement of the ship's bow, adjusting the helm to hold a steady course. We may not make much headway for the time being.

In extreme situations we must heave to and simply ride each big wave as it comes, as best we can. If we allow ourselves to be driven off course then we might become lost for a while in the rain and the mist. Precious time and resources may be spent getting ourselves back onto our heading once more. We may have lost position and so will need to make up time to recover our schedule.

We are sure you will agree, my friend, that emotional storms can cause us to feel great stress and in the most extreme circumstances they can even make us ill. At times, the waves of emotional energy which hit us can seem to be so solid and heavy that often we may feel physically battered much as a sailor at sea can become exhausted by the constant pounding of the seas against his ship.

Whence comes this stormy energy which can batter us so? Whence comes the great gales of anger, the hurricanes of hatred and the typhoons of violence? Whence comes the squalls of argument, the fogs of despair and the thin mists of confusion and disorientation?

We might say that humans live within an atmosphere of emotional energy in the same way that they live in the physical atmosphere of oxygen, nitrogen and the other gases. Although invisible to us, if the natural balance is changed then we can be profoundly affected. If oxygen levels are reduced for example, we may faint or even die.

So we might say then that we can be influenced very strongly by this emotional energy which surrounds us. We have all walked into a room and experienced the sense of a highly charged atmosphere.

In the same way that a tree breathes in carbon dioxide and breathes out oxygen, so do we absorb the emotions of others and express our emotional energy out towards them. Usually we are not conscious of this exchange, but we *are* aware of how it affects our feelings.

Let us say that a person has an angry outburst and energy is given off to this emotional atmosphere. Where does all this anger go? Great clouds of like energy will gather together, to create an energy field of anger. And in the same way great clouds of happiness and joy are also created, which gather together about this earth.

And now consider another person who is beginning to lose their temper and who draws unknowingly upon this reservoir of angry energy. They may feel a sudden burst of anger erupt deep within themselves and perhaps they may even lose control completely.

It could be said that the weather systems upon this earth are directly affected to some degree by these emotional energy fields. And so therefore, we can see how beneficial it might be to focus upon our stillness within. To stay calm and thus help to create an atmosphere of clarity, tranquillity and peace for ourselves and for the animals. And also for all the plants and for Mother Earth herself.

May the sunshine in your heart radiate out into the World

Resistance

Consider, if you will, a length of electrical wire connected to a charged battery. An electric current is said to flow from the higher potential to the lower. The strength of current is said to be governed by the voltage, the difference in electrical potential across the two opposite ends of the wire, which are interchangeable. We would say that this is a scientific fact. That it is real.

But if the piece of wire is disconnected it simply lies inert upon the table. So where has the electricity gone? Yes, the electrical current is real, it exists. It is a fact. But therefore, is it not an event? Is it not something which happens? So we can say then that electricity is an event which happens and when a wire is connected to an electrical circuit then electricity happens to be. It is *caused* to happen. It is an effect after the cause.

It is also a fact that when an electrical current flows in a wire then that wire becomes hot, it happens to be that the wire heats up. The stronger the current, then the hotter becomes the metal of the wire. It would seem to be that the molecules of the metal itself become more energised and they begin to vibrate at a faster rate than is normal. This then, is known as *resistance*.

Let us now consider two people who connect together. Two people who join together and engage in an argument. It happens now and then, does it not? Usually as the argument proceeds, so then does the conversation begin to heat up and often the words will begin to flow at an ever increasing speed.

We could say that the greater the difference of opinion between the two, then the more heated will become the discussion. Clearly, we can see that this event is an example of *resistance*. The greater their opposition to each other, then the greater the potential for a heated argument to erupt. If the argument is protracted, they may become exhausted and find themselves unable to continue the event.

Eventually, the two protagonists may burn out. The spark of energy which first inflamed the situation fades away and we could say that the electrical charge of the moment has gone. It is as if a fuse has blown and both have now become inert with fatigue.

So the argumentative individuals then are each resisting the point of view of the other. Sparks fly as a result of the natural laws of the universe and cause and effect creates an electric charge of energy, which flows between them.

And the greater the potential difference across the two perspectives then the greater is the flow of energy generated. It is said that water always finds its own level. And it does, does it not? So then, in like manner, is the potential equalised and the electrical charge is now gone. The flow of words ceases to be.

Often after an argument, people will say that they lost control, that they reacted spontaneously in the heat of the moment. Perhaps it is not surprising this is so, especially when we consider the fact that the most fundamental law of creation is at work here. It is at work everywhere.

So when two people begin to argue, forces are set in motion which are far greater than they could ever imagine. They are the *same* forces which move the planets about the sun and which cause to rotate great galaxies of stars in the firmament of outer space.

My Word! It really is no wonder then, that so often many find it almost impossible to resist arguing when the potential is there for it to happen. They have little comprehension of what is *really* going on and they cannot help themselves. Quite simply, once they have started then they just cannot stop!

If we push against anything it is law that it always pushes back

Responsibility

So it would seem that when two people engage in an argument, they are at the mercy of forces outside of their control. It would seem that they are unable to change the course of events. Perhaps we might say that it is their destiny. The situation *is* what it *is* and they cannot change what *is* about to happen. This is what most people might call their fate, is it not?

To experience something which they cannot control, something which they cannot prevent or change. So fate then, is something which cannot be altered and could be said to be predetermined in nature. What will happen, will happen.

Thus when two opponents square up for a verbal boxing match it is inevitable that it will take place. They are both looking for a fight and they will get one. It is useless for either to resist the situation because it is going to happen anyway. Once the starting bell has rung the fight will begin and there will be a winner and a loser, unless both first collapse with exhaustion.

We would say that if you hold a predetermined view of your reality then that view will become your reality. In other words, if you think that something is inevitable then truly will it be so. We are made in the image of God. We are creators.

Thus if we hold an image within our mind, so then will that image eventually come to be. If we hold true to a particular vision, so then will that vision come to be. It might be said to be predetermined and this is a truth.

It has been determined beforehand that it shall be so and thus it *is*. If you hold the view that within a given situation an argument is inevitable, then so will it be. You have predetermined what will happen by your vision of what will happen and the universal forces will begin to work in your favour.

They will do everything they can to help you to create your vision. The argument you see before you will indeed happen and once the forces have been set in motion your fate is sealed. It will happen. For you have made it so.

It is as if we have created a ball and set it rolling, downhill. The *laws of motion* now take over. If we have put enormous effort into our enterprise and created a huge ball, so then will it be that much more difficult to stop once it is rolling. The heavier the ball, then the more is the effort required to overcome inertia to get things on the move. And so therefore, is much more effort required to alter the outcome, if afterwards we decide to change our mind.

We might say then that the more thought we give to something, the more momentum do those thoughts carry and thus the more the inevitability of those thoughts becoming a reality. Sometimes, we might think similar thoughts so often that they become a habit of thought. We repeat the same thoughts over and over within our mind and so might we then create the same reality, over and over again. We are creators. And with our thoughts we make our world.

Perhaps we might say we have no choice in the matter. For how can we react otherwise to events in our lives? It is what life is and it is inevitable that we must put up with it. 'I can't change things!' you say. 'It's who I am!' you say. 'What can I do about it?' you say.

We would say that as creators, we do have the free will to change everything. If we so wish, we have the free will to make something new happen. All we need to do is to put some thought into it. We can imagine a fresh new image, of both ourselves and of the life that we live. We have the ability to create change in our lives.
So give it some thought, my friend. And see what happens....

As creators we always have a choice

Creativity

You have the ability to choose to make things happen, do you not? And thus can you create by the action of making things. You are a creator. The everyday action of simply walking is, in principle, exactly the same as the building of a large urban city such as London. It is the action of making something happen, is it not?

If you look about you, then will you see amazing human creativity everywhere. A creativity which seems to be ever expanding and growing, does it not? A creativity which seems to be a wonderful and marvellous physical phenomena.

We would say that yes, the results of human creativity are indeed physical in nature and that the evidence is all around you. But we would remind you, that everything first starts life as a thought. Therefore, we would say to you that human creativity is the *cause* and the creation which follows is the *effect*. That the creativity is the action and the creation which follows is the reaction.

Picture, if you will, in your mind's eye the carousel once more. It is a mighty structure, gaily painted and with many coloured lights. Music is playing. An engine is working at its centre to make the merry-go-round-go-round. Made of steel and wood, it has been created by craftsmen who have so diligently applied their crafts. And all of this we could say is very much a physical endeavour. It is a physical machine. It is made of physical materials and it is fashioned by physical effort.

Consider now a potter at his wheel, who takes a great delight in moulding the clay in order to create something physical. He is making a pot, the size and design of which begins to take shape first within his mind. It is the creation of his thought. However, the pot itself is made of clay which comes from the ground of Mother Earth.

So therefore, we might say that the physical reality of the pot has *already* been created. Perhaps then it is the *idea* of the pot which is the result of human creativity and not the physical pot itself.

It seems as though Mother Earth creates and provides for us a fully stocked kitchen and restaurant, wherein we may create culinary delights for both ourselves and others. Each chef, as the creator of their dish, is free to choose any ingredient and to use any piece of equipment. And they will do so according to their individual tastes and desires.

We are allowed to play. We can invent anything as we may so wish. But we must also learn, however, not to burn our fingers in the fat, boil dry the vegetables or give to our dinner guests food poisoning. It is as if we are born into Mother Earth, whereby we may learn and grow to be the budding super-chefs that we truly are.

Supplies and resources are unlimited. Working together as a team, we are free to create a ten course banquet for two hundred guests. Or we may choose instead to work alone and create a simple little dish of fruit salad for one lucky person. It is as though Mother Earth is a benevolent business woman, who has created an Establishment just for us and who is happy to give us all a free rein. To give us all the freedom to play and experiment with everything that is on offer and available for our use.

Human creativity is a *creative process of ideas*, ever expanding into new creation. Picture this, if you will. We are the artists, who have been given our palette of paints from God and we are free to paint our thoughts, our ideas, our images and our visions onto the canvas of our lives.... *Colour* and *Sound* made form in perfect harmony.

Reality is the reflection of our thought

A Game of Tennis

Have you ever been daydreaming? Have you ever been lost in thought? Have you ever looked out of a window at the clouds, yet seen them not? Maybe you have been to a big sporting event and became so engrossed in what was going on that you were unaware of the people around you.

Perhaps you have been to the cinema to watch a film and as you became so caught up in the story you were, for a time, oblivious to your surroundings. How can you totally lose yourself in something? Forsooth, hast thou lost thy mind and become lost to this world?

It does not seem to matter whether we are actively engaged in the physical sense, or not. When we experience a film at the pictures we are sitting still in a chair, yet we become involved actively in a mental or emotional sense. We are motionless but not e-motionless.

We seem to lose ourselves when we are involved in something. The word *involve* comes from a Latin verb which means to roll. When we roll ourselves into something then we become wrapped up or enfolded in it. We join with it. We experience it. We participate and so do we become *involved* in whatever we put our attention to.

If we are playing in a game of tennis, we can become so *involved* that we *are* that game of tennis. And to an observer, this would be a truth. Indeed, if you were not present and playing in that game then it would not exist, it would not *be*. 'But I'm a human being and not a game of tennis!' you say.

When we put our focus of attention upon something, do we not also turn our thoughts towards that something? Whatever it is, that we are doing? Do we not put our mind to it? And if our reality is a reflection of our thoughts, so must we *be* whatever we are doing. We become whatever we are doing.

'But that's ridiculous!' you say. 'Surely I must still be me!' you say. 'How can I become something else?' you say. 'But then that means I am not being myself!' you say. And we would agree. We would say that many people are, indeed, not being themselves.

They are their job, their career or profession. They are the family parent or grandparent. They are their hobbies and their favourite pastimes. So we could say, therefore, that they seem to exist only within their lives. That they *are* their lives.

We might say that many people never ever stop to take a look at themselves. Forever caught up in the moment of doing things, they are never still. They came to experience life and they jolly well shall do so. And quite right, too!

But if they are continuously playing that game of tennis, then they might experience exhaustion perhaps, sooner or later. They may collapse and become ill, requiring hospital care. And within this enforced idleness, so shall they begin to see themselves once more.

But they are not happy, doing *nothing*. It is uncomfortable for them to be still and be more aware, perhaps, of who they *are*. And now they find that they are a human *being*, instead of a human *doing*. Suddenly, they have lots of time. Time to reflect upon things. Time to think. To be thoughtful. To be calm. Be peaceful. Be still.

Rather like the interval between sets of games in tennis, we need a time to rest. To take stock of who we are and where we are going in life. To remember that we are the person doing the doing and not just the doing itself. To remember that we are observing ourselves playing the game of tennis, at the same time as we are playing it.

Be oneself and still play the game

A World of Thought

Have you ever been daydreaming? Have you ever been lost in thought? Have you ever looked out of a window at the clouds, yet seen them not? And did someone, perhaps, shout out at you? To tell you to *'Pull your socks up!'* To tell you to *'Stop dreaming and get real!'* To tell you to *'Put your feet on the ground!'*

To that other person, you do indeed seem to be lost within your own world. From their perspective, you really do not appear to be living in the same reality as they are. And you are not. For you are living within *your* world of thoughts and you perceive *your* reality from within that world of your own imagination. We can say that each and every one of us sees this world around us from our own very unique point of view.

And if we but reflect awhile, then we must surely all agree that truly do we live within the world of our *own* thoughts. For how can it be otherwise? How can we live inside the head of someone else? How on earth can we possibly live within the world of another person's thoughts? Indeed, we would agree that it is impossible because we can only perceive our reality from within our own personal perspective.

But we would also agree, however, that you do indeed live within a world of the thoughts of other people. Are you sitting right now within a building? A construction which you did not conceive or design? A construction which you did not build, fit out or furnish? If so then you are living now, at this very moment, within another world. The world of someone else.

You are living quite literally within their thoughts, made real from their minds. You are living within a reality which came from their imagination. You are living in a world of *their* thoughts.

And those thoughts do not have to be so solid and real about you. Consider the world of politics. Is this not a world of words and policy? Of ideals and treachery? We could say that this is a world of ideas and not things. And so, therefore, that it is not so real. Yet countries go to war over politics and that is real enough.

My Word! This is all so confusing, is it not? Best to try and keep a clear head then. So where is the dividing line separating us from the world? It would seem that we are living in our own minds and yet also in the minds of others, too. How can we make sense of all this?

Perhaps it is time that we looked at what a thought actually *is*. But if there is no time, how then can we grasp the notion of a thought? In a flash, it seems to just come from *nothing*. It seems to just come and go, so maybe we can say that it is a product of our imagination. If emotion is the energy of *thought* in motion, then maybe thought is the energy of our *mind* in motion.

Consider once again the emotional atmosphere within which we live. That energy has been generated from the many different ways in which we all think and respond to our world. Therefore we might say then that we live within *an atmosphere of thought energy*. Have you ever been swept up in the momentum of a great crowd and just had to go with it? As if you had been like a small cork, floating on a great wave of motion and emotion, energy in motion.

So if we think of our thoughts as *mind energy* in motion, then we can say that we are all living within a *Great Sea of Thoughts* and as those thoughts interact in waves of cause and effect, so do they create our reality.

Waves of eternal thought roll in upon the beach of our mind

A World of Nature

If the nature of this world be thought then so also must thought be the nature of this world. That is a most natural conclusion to reach, is it not? 'Why naturally so!' you may say. 'No need to think about that really!' you say. 'It's only natural!' you say. And to be honest, judging by the *nature* of things as they stand at the moment, it is a sound argument, is it not? Indeed, an argument best not to resist.

Go with the flow then, no point in getting hot and bothered about it. There is, after all, a most natural flow to everything in nature, is there not? There is an easy vitality which just seems to be. Life goes on. Individuals come and go but the nature of nature remains unchanged.

Or does it? On the face of it, nature does indeed seem to stay the same. And much like the laws of the universe it is a constant reality in our lives. But, of course, we know from facts gathered by many scientists that nature does indeed change slowly over the years.

Now this does make sense. At last, something seems to make some sense. We know that thought never seems to stop or to stand still. And now we also know that the nature of this world is thought. Therefore it must be so that nature never stands still.

And we cannot argue with that statement, can we? We know that we can try to resist nature. We can try to push it back. But when we stop and stand still, so then does nature come back again. It just keeps on sort of growing really, in a very natural sort of way.

But what of nature itself? Is it not a most marvellous creation of life? It is so complex and everything seems to be interconnected in some way. So well thought out we can say. And we would be right. For it is plain to see that life is intelligent.

No matter which small part of nature we may choose to look at, we see that there is behind that nature an intelligence at work and that intelligence is, perhaps, far greater than the lesser intellects of mere humans. The more we look then the more we see. Nature is truly incredible and a most wonderful creation, is it not?

Nature is indeed so well made, almost as if it has been designed. It has been said that Archangels are the *Engineers of the Universe*. And it is obvious to anyone who looks closely enough, that nature has been engineered to perfection.

Like the well designed engine of a motor vehicle, all the moving parts fit together and work together for the purpose of being itself. An engine which works in conjunction with the rest of the motor vehicle, also complete in itself. It stands ready and fit for purpose, perhaps to take the driver to work or to the supermarket.

So nature then fits together perfectly for the purpose of being itself. And of itself, it is naturally perfect. It is ever changing but always working together in a perfect rhythm of movement of colour and sound made form.

Can you hear it? Like a car engine, it has a vibrational hum. It is so subtle, however, that you might need to use your second sight to see it and your clairaudience to hear it.

The harmonic of *Nature's Song* is smooth and melodious, although sometimes a note may seem to fall a little flat to our ears because we are not yet fully attuned to the majesty of the full sound and colour of the *Great Orchestral Symphony*.

May we yearn to know the nature of God's Love

The Nature of Fear

Fear is experienced when we desperately want to stop something
from happening and we cannot. It is as if we need to stop the
carousel and get off. But we are not able to achieve this feat. In fact,
it is impossible for anyone or anything to stop the carousel.

'But why not!' you say. Because my friend, you just simply cannot
stop the universe. The momentum of energy at work is so vast that
it could be said to be infinite in nature. We cannot stop the carousel.

So we resist. We try to stop it or at least try to slow it down. But the
great engine at the heart of this carousel is mighty. It is well made,
perfectly engineered we might say. It is well designed and well
thought out indeed. We cannot stop creation from happening.
It is the universal law. It is the will of God.

So we resist. We still try to stop it or at least try to slow it down.
Even though we are aware of the impossibility of this feat. So we
might say then that fear is a reflex action, an automatic reaction to
a stimulus. Sometimes, we just simply cannot stop ourselves from
resisting a given situation. It is as if the law of cause and effect is
working both for us and against us. An impossible situation then.

So we resist. And like the wire in the electrical circuit we get hot.
We get stressed. We seem to vibrate at a faster rate than normal.
Sometimes so much so that we can become drained of physical
energy and then cannot continue onwards. We faint. We freeze.
Sometimes people have even died of fright.

So we resist. But the forces at work are so powerful that we cannot
win. No matter what we will, it cannot be. We feel so powerless.
We feel so weak. In that moment of fear does it seem as if the
whole of the universe is against us.

So we resist. And in that moment do we feel alone. Do we feel that we are doomed to failure. Do we feel that urgent need to survive at whatever cost.

So we resist. And we fail. It is said that the only fear that we need to fear is the fear of fear itself. Truly is this so, because that fear is trying to achieve an impossible feat. And so we find ourselves in a situation which we cannot win. What then can we do?

Surrender. We must let go. Our inner wisdom tells us that in order to deal with the immediate circumstances, then we must let go and become still. Only within that stillness do we see a solution to the problem. As if we realise that the carousel will just keep on moving and we have decided to stop trying to stop it.

Instead do we move towards the inner stillness, where we no longer feel distress and fear has no control over us. We find that we now have a clarity of mind and feel calm. From *within* can we observe the problem and with *insight* and understanding find a solution.

Have you ever experienced a moment of extreme danger, when time seems to slow down or even stop? A moment when suddenly you feel totally calm and almost serene, with a sense of the utmost clarity of mind. You feel no fear. You seem to have almost super-human abilities and thus are you able to save yourself from harm.

The physical reflex of fear has gone because in that *moment* you have become the observer, rather than the participant who is in danger. Fear could be said to be a physical experience, associated with the need of the body to survive. And so when we observe ourselves from within our inner perspective, shall we feel no fear.

Trust and know in your heart that all is well

Survival

When a circumstance has become inevitable, then must we learn to trust and surrender ourselves to it. If we observe life closely then we might see that when a small prey has been caught by a predator, a moment may come when it knows that there is to be no escape.

It surrenders to the moment. With great wisdom and trust it will choose to let go of its physical life. In that moment of surrender to *God's Great Love* it knows no fear, only stillness. In that moment of truth does it know that all is well.

When a great tree is felled, a berry picked from a bush or a blade of grass trampled underfoot, so also do they surrender to the moment. Do they let go of physical life. Do they become still and trust in *God's Great Love*. Do they know in that moment of truth, that all is well.

Sooner or later, humans find that they too have a need to submit to the moment of death. To surrender the physical body, giving it back to Mother Earth. That they too have a need to let go and to trust in *God's Great Love*. In that moment of truth, do they know no fear. And in the stillness do they know all is well.

When a rock is put into a great furnace and smelted, does it know fear? Probably not. When a plant is pulled from the ground and put into a shredder, does it know fear? Probably not, although it will experience briefly some distress. When a human is confronted by imminent death, do they know fear?

Probably, yes. Before they surrender to the moment of truth. We might say that only humans feel lack of ease about when or where or how it may happen. Only humans fear dying. But why should this be so? For in truth, we most assuredly do survive the moment.

Is it all to do with a lack of trust perhaps? For plants and animals question not. Does not questioning itself sometimes promote a feeling of distrust and scepticism? Deep within, we all know and trust in *God's Great Love*. So where does this lack of trust come from?

Doubt created by human intellect must be to blame for this fear, which says that only the physical body exists and that when it dies, so do we also. We would say yes, that the body is of the physical form but your *feeling* is not, your *thought* is not, your *mind* is not, thus when you die your body is not, but *you are*.

Humans tend to create a stronger personal identity in a sense that maybe other life forms do not. The intellect is a product of human personality, is it not? And this identity is *thought* based. It has to be because we create with our thoughts, do we not? Our personalities then, are thought forms.

We could say that it is not death itself we fear but the thought of death, the *idea* that we do not survive. We create an image of death within our minds which is not real. We imagine death to be the end when in reality, it is not. Some people even fear survival, they have perhaps created within their minds vivid images of an everlasting torment or eternal boredom.

If we observe these thoughts with clarity and understanding, then we can see that they are but the creation of the human imagination and thus a by-product of this physical life. For most truly, in death do we become alive again to *God's Great Love* and we know once more our truth.

Verily do we say unto thee that there is only life

The Schoolroom

Imagine yourself, if you will, sitting once again at a desk in school. It is a glorious day and the sun is shining. Next to a window, you are free to look outside at the beautiful scenery at any time you so choose whilst the class is in progress. You are free to reflect for as long as you may wish upon the words spoken by the teacher, who as yet has not arrived. You are free to be yourself.

As everyone eagerly awaits for the lesson to begin, the room is very noisy and you can feel the keen excitement of your classmates. You look around and are surprised to find that you recognise most of your fellow pupils, especially as you don't remember ever coming to school before. It seems to be the first day, but you are not sure really. It is certainly a new day though.

You see members of your family and many old friends, as well as some new ones. It will be fun to talk and catch up with everyone during the break. You feel comfortable and relaxed. No one seems to know what the lesson will be about nor how long it will be, but you are all joyfully anticipating a wonderful time.

Sitting there, you glance out of the window and begin to recall your parents, who together with some older members of the family had seen you off on your way. They had explained everything to you about school and why you were going today. You know there is a purpose but you cannot remember it, as there was just far too much to try and take in at the time.

And so here you are, after waving goodbye to them all. They had given you a packed lunch in your new satchel and proudly brushed your brand new school uniform with love. And they had given you some last minute instructions, telling you to behave yourself and to pay attention to everything that goes on. To enjoy yourself, because school is such fun. There is so much to experience and learn about life.

They told you not to worry. That they are only a thought away and to think of them often. That they will assist you in your homework if you ever need any help with things. You remember that you had playfully asked them to help you cheat with some of the answers but they had just laughed and said no. There would be no point to it they had said, for you would only have to repeat the whole lesson again if you took any short cuts.

The classroom falls silent. Everyone is waiting. Teacher begins to appear before us, clothed in a long white robe shimmering gently in a soft golden light. Smiling a warm greeting, words are spoken without a sound. Eyes shining bright with wisdom and knowledge, upon the head you see perched incongruously a black mortar board worn at a rakish angle. Everyone laughs and Teacher smiles, *today I am wearing my teacher's hat.*

The school register appears and Teacher begins to read out names to the class. Hearing your name spoken you don't recognise it, but you do like the sound of it. It's a new name.

At last, Teacher declares *the lesson is starting.* On the desk in front of you a small book appears. You try to open it but the pages seem to be stuck together. Like all your classmates, you pick it up and wonder what to do with it. What's it for? Teacher hears the question and gives an answer to the whole class straightaway, *this is the school curriculum and timetable, a master is allowed to open it but only with permission from the headmaster.*

A second book now appears with your new name upon the cover. Opening itself to the first page, you see that it is blank. But as you look, words are now beginning to be written upon it....

The story of my life. Am I sitting comfortably?
Good. Then I shall begin....

The Playground

We go to school and whilst there we may enjoy or endure lesson after lesson. And of what do we learn? Some of this and some of that. Some of that and some of this. We learn to conform. We learn to be a good pupil. We learn about human society and the world. We learn to be a good citizen. Yet the most important lesson of all is missed by so many and often goes unnoticed.

Year after year, we get older and older and the teachers work very hard to teach us all to work very hard. We learn that work is a good thing. We learn that work is something which adults do. We learn that to gain exam results then so must we work hard. We learn, in fact, that life is about work, work and more work. Now where on earth is the fun in all that?

Gradually, life becomes mostly hard work. We work hard and we play hard. And to play hard is hard work indeed, is it not? It is no wonder then that so many of us get stressed, grow old, fall ill and die and not always in that particular order. So often life becomes responsibilities, money, family, career, status, wealth or the lack of it and health or the lack of it. So often have we missed the most important lesson of all, the lesson of the playground.

It is a lesson not learned in the classroom. In fact, it is not a lesson at all. It is not something of which we have a need to learn for it is something we *already* know. Instinctively, do we all understand this great truth. It cannot be taught to us. It is something *we are*.

Consider what happens when we go to school. What is it that we *really* learn? What is it that shapes our future? Perhaps we should look at the word *school* itself. We find that it is not only a place of learning, but also is used in the sense of a group of people who share the same ideas. So schooling is, in essence, about learning a particular set of ideas and how to think of them in a certain way.

At first sight, we might think that our education is about learning to grow up and think for ourselves, to help us to become an adult. To help us to become independent. And to some extent, this is indeed a truth. However, we are learning to live the thoughts of *other* people. We learn to accept *their* truth as *our* truth. In other words, we learn to be not *our*selves but *them*selves.

'We learn about facts and things that are useful!' you may say. 'I can learn to grow as an individual!' you say. 'I am always me!' you say. Nevertheless, we would say to you that the only reason your life might become hard work is because you are trying to live the lives of others. Trying to be, as *they* are. But you are, as *you* are.

You cannot, with satisfaction, be someone else and even if you do manage this feat you will be unhappy simply because you are not being yourself. We could say that it takes a great deal of effort not to be yourself. It takes hard work and a lot of it.

Consider the animals. Do they work hard? No! They learn through playing and they live just as themselves. We would say that they experience well-being unless, perhaps, they have contact with the human world. They know who they are. They think for themselves.

When in the school playground, we are free from the thought forms of established education. We are free to be more ourselves. We are free to play and we are free to laugh. *We are free spirits*.

We think you will find that the most successful people are happier, more fulfilled and often wealthier simply because they are free thinkers and so choose to live their own lives.

Try to be yourself more and have some fun

Balance

Consider a man walking along a high-wire which stretches out tight between two tall buildings. Perhaps you have watched early black and white film of just such an event, maybe from the 1920's. These death defying stunts very aptly illustrate that which we wish to discuss with you now.

He carries a long balancing pole to help him to stay upright, whilst strong gusts of wind attempt to push him off the wire. At the same time this wire beneath his feet is also moving, swaying from side to side. The gentleman in question keeps a clear head with a strong attentive focus as he walks along the taut steel cable. He would have given up a short prayer to God before setting out. Indeed, it is always wise to try and predetermine an outcome when danger is involved!

We would say to you that *everyone* maintains just such a balancing act, in every moment of their lives. For life events external to your immediate being will often attempt to push your ship of life off course and may even cause you to lose your emotional or mental balance. Cause you to shift your point of focus. Sometimes, direct physical events can attempt to knock you over causing you to lose your balance and to fall.

When your ship of life is steaming through a heavy swell perhaps or experiencing rough weather, it is wise to follow the example of the sailors at sea in this physical world. They always keep their eyes fixed upon the distant horizon. Their point of focus is always upon the stillness and so do they never lose their sense of inner balance. It is only when people fix their focus upon the movement of the ship instead, that they will get seasick or fall over.

'Never look down!' people often say. How true this saying is. For when we look down, especially from any great height, so often do we cause ourselves to lose our balance.

When we look down, we see an immediate image in our minds of where we do *not* want to go. And so we fall. For with our thoughts do we not create our reality? The gentleman on the high-wire always looks ahead and never does he shift his gaze downwards.

He focuses upon a distant point and thus does he maintain his inner balance. In so doing, does he maintain his sense of physical balance also. As the wind attempts to push him first in one direction and then another, so does he automatically adjust the weight of the pole to compensate the forces of cause and effect at work.

The pole is always held in the middle, like the piece of wood with two ends. And in that middle, just like the carousel, do we find the stillness and the centre of our being. We all live immersed within the *Great Sea of Thoughts* around us and so then do we need to maintain our mental balance. So too, must we maintain emotional balance as we live within the emotional atmosphere around us.

But how on earth are we to cope with everything that's going on? How can we stay aware of all the forces which are at work? Our thoughts and emotions are invisible! It isn't possible to concentrate totally in every single moment! If we can't look down then how do we know how high up we are? It's not possible to monitor each and every thought or emotion!

We would say that you should follow the example of the sailor at sea and the gentleman on the wire. Try to keep focused upon your distant goal and your inner stillness, always try to look in the same direction that you are travelling and thus will you maintain your balance automatically. You will not need to think about it all the time. For God has, indeed, truly thought of everything.

Stay on course and keep a good lookout as you plough ahead through the waves

Reflection

Let us reflect my friend, for a moment, upon the idea once more of two people who engage in an argument. Picture, if you will, the situation within your mind. See it clearly in your mind's eye. Each person starts to raise their voice to try to be heard above the other. Like tennis balls in a game of tennis, words are being hit hard into the air. Some strike their intended target, others do not. Points are scored. Physical exertion takes place.

At first sight, they would seem to be in opposition to each other. However, since there is in truth no such thing as an opposite, then something else must be happening here. Perhaps we are witnessing instead an energy flow between two people. This is an everyday occurrence which we all take for granted. It happens, momentarily, everywhere and to everybody. Naturally enough, energy just flows. Although this particular type of event does seem to stand out it is, nevertheless, only a simple energy flow.

There are no opposites, only relative position. So we are a witness to a flow of energy from a higher potential to a lower, much as a waterfall equalises the relative position of two bodies of water. The two protagonists are each standing in a different position. Indeed, if they were standing together *as one*, there would be no argument. But they are separated by disagreement. Both are looking directly at each other, yet cannot see eye to eye on anything.

And so do the laws of physics take over and in the same way that a waterfall happens, so does an argument take place. Indeed, nothing else can take its place. The relative position of the two bodies both *involved* has predetermined the event and the outcome is assured. The law of cause and effect is thus being expressed in a natural and normal way. It always is. And so the two individuals, seemingly in separate positions, are joined together in a flow of energy in order for the situation to become balanced once more.

Like the waterfall, it happens because the circumstance is required to resolve itself. So words fly back and forth. They are spoken or shouted out loud with a charge of emotional energy behind them. They *are* the expression of emotion. People arguing are expressing themselves emotionally and this energy then dissipates to the emotional atmosphere where it collects together as an energy field, until it gradually fades away.

So as we reflect and ponder upon this situation which we can see so clearly within our minds, we might say that there is no reflection going on here. The words spoken are in opposition to each other. However, energy flow needs to be equal and opposite in order for the argument to resolve itself and potential to come into balance.

So the words flow from Left to Right and from Right to Left. And like the two ends of the piece of wood, they are equal and opposite in nature. As the two oppositely charged ends of a magnet are still both part of the same magnet so, in like manner, are the opposing polarities of argument both part of the same energy field.

The two people are inseparably joined together in argument. To an observer, they *are* the one event but the participants see themselves as separate from each other. So we could say that the opposition is only mental in nature and exists within their minds only. We might say that a person who is arguing is a person mentally challenged.

They are experiencing an opposite viewpoint, *a reflection*, of their own mental position. Each is seeing a living image of themselves, an embodiment, being reflected back to them. But it is a mirror image and the viewpoint has become reversed. With our thoughts do we make our world and so is our reality made real about us in every moment. Be at peace, my friend and so will you live in peace.

We see ourselves reflected in the life around us

Light

So what do you make of all this so far, my friend? Are you able to make anything at all? Have you been able to create images in your mind, of these words and the meanings of these words? Or, is it all still as clear as mud to you? Maybe you just need to give the mud a chance to settle, until you have some clarity once more.

Take a break then and relax. Just *be*. Clear your mind of everything. Allow your mind to settle. Do not stir up the muddy sediment of all your old memories and ideas. Let the silt of your past thoughts lie still and inert, upon the seabed of your *Sea of Thoughts.*

Allow then that sea to become calm and still. Allow your mind to be still. Let it be. Just be. For a moment and a moment and another moment. It all seems to blur into one. One moment. One reality. *One eternal truth of being.*

So, take a break. Relax and enjoy the moment. Perhaps it is time now to make *light* of it all and to have some fun. And then maybe will the muddy *Sea of Your Thoughts* become clearer to you. And to have some light amusement is always a good idea, so allow then the magic of the Muses to enlighten you.

When we are enjoying ourselves, we do not seem to think about things so much, do we? We live more in the moment and so time seems to fly by, does it not? Joyfully, we take things as they come. Everything just seems to flow and time has no meaning.

So relax then and enjoy the moment, a timeless moment. And if time has no meaning for you, then so must you also be timeless. So must *you* be eternal. And when you are in a moment of joy, you are being you. Your *eternal self*. Your beingness. Your highness. And when you are not enjoying yourself, you feel low and you are being your lowness instead of your highness.

Your eternal self is *joy*. When you are being your lowness, so then are you not being your *self*. When you react to events which cause you to lose touch with your joy, so then do you feel low. When you give attention to things which are not joyful, so then are you low. You are no longer *being* your joy but you are *being* something else.

You may have put your focus on a reality of the physical echoes of thoughts past, memories of past moments. You might also have created in your mind strong ocean currents, which have stirred up sediments from the seabed and so old thoughts are now repeating themselves.

So, of what are you thinking in this very moment? Thoughts from the past or images of what is to come? Past creation or a vision of the future? Are you looking ahead of you or are you looking down at the mud? Are you living within past moments or the present moment? Is your glass half full or half empty? And is it clear or muddy?

To see anything clearly, we need light. We need illumination to see if we have clear presence of mind, or not. So have you some clarity yet? Is your mind clear enough to see the sunlight being reflected back to you as you hold up your glass to the *Blue Skies of Heaven*? Can you see beautiful and radiant vibrant waves of indescribably iridescent colours of the *Light*?

Can you see the sparkle of sunlight yet? Can you *feel* it within your heart? When we focus upon the light, so do we *become* that light. It is reflected within our *being*. And like a lighthouse, we are able to shine that light out to others. *Be the Light*. So enjoy your life, have fun and make light of it all.

See the sparkle of your light reflected in others

Integrity

So, my friend, how can we tie this all up in a satisfactory manner?
With a pretty pink bow perhaps? The answer is pretty obvious, is it
not? You should be able to see it coming, so shall we leave it until
we get to the end of this part of the book? You will then see if you
are clairvoyant, or not. You will know if you have clear knowing,
or not. You will feel if you have clairsentience, or not.

So, where were we then? Ah, yes, *now*. Well, in a word. *Integrity*.
You will need to find your integrity. When did you see it last?
Recently we hope. But what does it mean to have integrity?

Do you play the sport of golf? Have you ever hit the perfect shot?
Have you achieved *perfection* in the *game*? That is to say, have you
attained a *whole* in one? To reach this goal one must be upright and
perfectly balanced in stance, with a clear mind and a clear focus.
One must be wholly oneself, in the moment of *being*.

Does not this word mean the idea and the reality of wholeness? And
so we wish, therefore, to throw this word at you rather as if we were
throwing you a tennis ball, in the hope that you might catch what it
is that we are trying to say to you.

We throw this *integrity* at you because it represents and expresses
an idea, which we want you to reach for and grasp with both hands.
It is an idea which we wish to place into your mind and that is
communication, is it not? Thus we wish to communicate with you,
mind to mind. So no intellectual arguments here please. Just let go
and surrender to this moment. Surrender to *God's Great Love*.

And so, we throw this word at you with great gentleness and love.
You may resist if you wish, for you have the free will of a creator.
But we do so hope that together we can catch it softly. We give it to
you as a gift. We might say that it is a gift from God.

And in truth do we say also, that *everything* is God-given. Including these words which you are reading right now, in this very moment, printed upon this page before you.

We are communicating our thoughts to you as words, from outside of time. For we are speaking to you *now* in this very moment with these words, *mind to mind*. It is as though the moment these very words were first written down onto the page, is *now*. It is the same moment. It is *all* one moment. It is *all* now.

It is a gloriously sunny day with a brilliant blue sky as our thoughts are being put into words for you and for us, by our friend. Can you feel the warmth of the sun? Can you feel the warmth of our love? We communicate with you across time, as you know it to be. Can you feel our presence? For *we are here*, there is nowhere else to be, only *here* in the *here and now*.

We do so hope that you make more use of a dictionary now. For the words contained therein hold the ideas and thoughts of humankind. All of the knowledge is within your grasp, as you hold a dictionary. All you have to do is to put the words and the thoughts into the right order. If you so wish, you can use words to find and hold the key to unlock thoughts of eternal wisdom from the *Great Teachers*.

So, in a word. We wish to give to you.... *integrity*. But as the old saying goes, 'it takes one to know one.' And indeed it does. For to know *one*ness, then *one* must be *one*. Therefore, we can say that to know wholeness of being you will have need to find your integrity.

be still, be peace, be love,
be yourself, be joy,
be whole.

Verily in the oneness of being is all love

Evolution

So, my friend, what is it all about? What is the purpose of it all? Has our dissertation answered these questions for you? Perhaps not. Your conclusion so far might be to say that life is about having fun. But why? For what purpose? What is the point? It is far too simple an explanation, for life is much too complicated a phenomenon to be explained away by just a single word. And we would agree that it does seem to be so.

We wish for you to reflect, for a moment, upon memories of good times when you were having great fun. Picture, if you will, within your mind where you were, what you were doing and who you were with. Think about it deeply and you might just begin to realise that the sense of fun you experienced during those times was exactly the same, no matter where or what you were doing or with whom.

That sense of fun which you felt was, in fact, within yourself. It was something which you were actually being, rather than doing. We have already discussed the idea that your eternal self is joy. In other words we are saying that, quite simply, you *are* your joy. It is who you are and it is what you are. It matters not what activity you are currently engaged upon nor where you are in this great Universe. For always, deep within your being, is *joy*.

'But what has that got to do with ordinary life?' you say. 'Why do I feel miserable?' you say. 'Life is often full of pain and suffering!' you say. 'Where is the fun in that?' you say. 'It just doesn't add up!' you say. And you would be right, it does not. So what then is the answer to this most perplexing of conundrums?

We can say that your joy is within and your ordinary life is without. That your joy is always with you no matter what changes happen in your life. When you feel miserable your joy has not gone anywhere. It has not evaporated away into the emotional atmosphere. So, what is it then that is happening? The answer is simple.

The focus of your attention is now no longer your joy but is instead the earthly life. You react with feelings, as you live whatever you are doing and you have now become your life. You have become a *human being* and you are now unaware, of your *eternal being*.

Let us look once again, at the idea of the carousel. Creation is all about movement and activity, is it not? It is about the joy of making things happen, is it not? When we feel that joy so are we then being *conscious* of our inner self, that stillness which lies at the heart of the carousel.

We are, in truth, like the piece of wood with two ends which seem to be separate and yet are one and the same thing. We appear to be a part of creation, living in a physical body and experiencing life. Yet also are we apart from creation, as we observe all from within our inner being.

Life is never still and yet we can be still. Our greatest thrill then is to experience the best of both worlds. To feel and know a deep *joy* within at the same time as we live our physical life on Earth.

The carousel never stops. On-the-merry-go-round-of-life do we evolve our being, with our thoughts made reality. We are forever moving forward into the expansion of wonderful new experiences. Life itself *evolves*, it rolls out creatively into a glorious and most magnificent future. My Word! Just imagine that!

So, my friend, how can we tie this all up in a satisfactory manner? Well, in a word. *Consciousness*. Did you see that one coming? Yes? If you did then have a big Gold Star and a pretty pink bow perhaps. *To understand life so then do we need to understand consciousness*.

**There are 24 subjects in Part III. 24 is 2 + 4 giving 6
and 24 is a reflection of 42....**

PART IV

YET ANOTHER BEGINNING OF THIS BOOK

Life Bursts Forth

Whence comes the creative process of life, my friend? Does it come literally from out of the ether itself? From out of *nothing*? Does it appear from nowhere, to *now here*? Yes, we would say that it does. The *whole* thing, in fact, is quite magical.

We make a wish, cast a spell and so must it be. It is well worth studying traditional children's stories and fantasies for they often contain profound truths, dismissed by many adults as a nonsense.

Except ye be as a little child, ye cannot know *The Heavenly Glory*. We would say it is the children who hold the keys to understanding and not the adults. For it is the child who has the *sense* and the adult the *non-sense*, because the adult has developed an intellect.

We might say that this intellect is a structure of thought forms and these forms are then used to create yet more structures of thoughts. It is, if you will, a type of mental scaffolding used to build up new creative thought. It is used to *form* new ideas.

It could be said to be like an architect, who draws up plans of new houses to be built. A designer of ideas. A shaper of all the thoughts within our mind. Organising each fact after the fact of building the building. Thus do we manufacture and build our lives, moment by moment and day by day.

So the adult has created an intellect through a process of education which is used to structure their life. We can say this education has itself been created, by intellect. We can say also that different kinds of educational structures around the world have created various systems of belief. And the result is that people live their lives in many different ways. So it would seem then, as if our architects build us different designs of houses in different parts of the world. And they do, do they not?

So we could say that our life is designed by a thinker of thoughts within our mind. A creative designer who uses thought in the same way that a builder uses bricks, to build a house.

And if we look at houses which have been built, we can see how the style of thinking and the method of construction has changed over the years. The designs have *evolved*, have they not? Ideas have changed because thinking has changed. Life moves on and new creations come into form. Some better than others perhaps, more efficient and better designed.

If we think of the Dinosaurs, then we know that they are no longer created as a living life form upon the Earth. But we also know that certain principles of their design have been incorporated in animals of today. Scientists have found out that present day life forms have developed from those of earlier ages. We could say then, that life grows through experience.

Mother Earth has created for us this wonderful Establishment, this building so well designed and functional for our use. Budding super-chefs create new recipes in the kitchen, hidden from view of the diners in the restaurant. Occasionally is a new menu prepared, offering new creations for customers to experience. The Head Chef keeps a record of all the recipes, in the Office.

So *creative thinkers* form new ideas and recipes are drawn up. The ingredients are mixed and left to stand awhile. Then tested for flavour and adjusted to perfection until finally the buns are put into the oven. Cooking times will vary accordingly, until at last they are ready. And *new creations* burst forth upon Mother Earth. Is not life itself incubated and born out of new thinking and new ideas? *New thoughts made form*?

From consciousness does a thinker create new thought

Joyful Growth

Life grows then through experience. We can say, and your intellect will agree, that over millions of years life has developed on Mother Earth. Scientists observe that the universe is ever expanding and life it would seem never stands still. The carousel of creation just never stops turning. *Roll up! Roll up! For All the Fun of the Fair!*

Budding super-chefs are forever working away in unseen kitchens, producing recipes for new life experience. But not all the creations will make it to the restaurant table. It is a *health and safety* matter, of course. With form after form after form. New ideas need to be tried and tested before being made available to the customers.

Everything has to pass the inspection of the Head Chef before it is allowed to go onto the table menus. It is obvious, in the intellectual sense, that for a culinary delight to be successful then must all the ingredients work together to produce a well balanced dish.

Before anything can be served up for the enjoyment and satisfaction of a customer, great thought has to be put into it. Knowledge which has been learned through experience must be applied to ensure that the end result is a great success. That all the ingredients match and everything goes together well.

We can say then that life does not really appear from out of thin air. It *is* true however, that to a customer sitting at the table, it can seem miraculous perhaps when a waiter suddenly brings to them a fully created dish. But behind the scenes great effort has been expended in the kitchen to produce this creation.

Great minds have been at work to ensure that life on Mother Earth is fit for purpose and that *all* exists together within perfect harmony and balance. It is well thought out and designed, very much like the engine of a motor car. All the moving parts fit together perfectly for the purpose of driving the motor vehicle.

And the motor vehicle itself is fit for the purpose of allowing the car driver to move around, as they might wish. Life is not just a haphazard affair, coming together in some random sort of way as some intellectuals seem to think. Like the motor car, life has been designed. Truly, is it a great wonder then how everything all works together, for the good of *all* life.

It is most amazing, is it not? Life is beneficial and it is here for our delight, to experience new things and to grow in the *being* of it. Have you ever looked closely at a butterfly? Such a delicate beauty to behold, is it not? Such a joy to hold in your hand and the shape and the colour of the wings are a true wonder. And for what is the purpose, other than to express itself? To express the design and the perfection of creation. To express God's beauty.

Often we can take the life around us for granted. It is a *given* thing. We have not had to put any work into it, because someone else has. As you go about daily life driving in your motor car, you think not of the factory nor the labour which has produced it. You think not of the thoughts which have created the design. You think not of the great effort which has gone into the fact of building your motor car.

Do you not drive your physical body in the same manner that you drive your motor vehicle? Does not the body respond to your thoughts in the same way as your motor vehicle responds to your hands at the wheel?

Like the car, your body has been designed and created for your use. Is this not a most wonderful gift? Like the magnificent butterfly, your body is an expression of the creation and perfection of God's beauty. It is provided free for you to use, to live your life and grow joyfully within your being.

Be conscious as you drive your vehicle of life

Abundance

Consider, if you will, the bird upon the wing and the beast in the forest. Whence comes their food or shelter? We would say that Mother Nature provides for all their needs in each and every way. Is not the same also a great truth, for humans? Indeed, the plentiful and most bounteous *Nature of Mother Earth* abundantly provides everything which we might ever need or want.

Wherefore then cometh the idea of shortage or lack? Perhaps this concept is the result of a flawed education system. For people are taught to expect limitation and insufficiency. People are taught a truth which is, in truth, a non-truth. For we *all* live in a world of abundance. We could say then that this idea is the product of the human intellect. It is a belief system created by education.

Very few people indeed ever really question information which has been given to them. Knowledge handed down from one generation to the next is usually accepted as a truth. As we discussed earlier, school is not only about facts and figures but is also about teaching particular systems of belief. People are taught to look at the world about them and to interpret it in the normally accepted way.

'And what is so wrong with that?' you say. 'The animals teach their young and human society has advanced much through education!' you say. And yes, we would agree. But there is one fundamental difference, however, between the human world and the natural world. No limitation exists within the world of Mother Nature.

Everywhere we look we see an abundance of life and there is no shortage to be found in Nature. Life is bountiful and ever growing. The plants and animals live in the moment, adapting to changes of circumstance. They live without fear of limitation and whenever an apparent lack appears, for example a local drought perhaps, it is compensated for elsewhere. There exists a natural balance.

Consider once more the waterfall, equalising the relative position of two bodies of water. Energy will always flow naturally and thus between anything is the relative difference of abundance or lack a temporary condition only always resolving itself in the end. Indeed, it cannot be otherwise.

So we can say that whatever abundance or lack a human observer might see in the natural world, it is but a momentary circumstance in the eternal ebb and flow of the effects of cause and as the moon creates the tides upon the ocean so does the universal law create the conditions of life upon Mother Earth.

Humans observe a temporary situation and with their intellect they then create a belief. A truth within their own minds that shortage and limitation must exist within this World. So a dam is built and water collected. Excess food is produced and crops stored. Land is misused, nature abused and natural resources are squandered.

The natural ebb and flow of events is altered in the short term by human intervention. Flow of energy is temporarily affected by the actions of millions of people on earth and so then does the human world begin to experience in reality those very shortages and limitations it so fears. Cause and effect is at work in the world.

Humans have created their own shortages, for they no longer live their lives in harmony with Mother Nature. Essentially food *grows for free*, naturally. It is not rocket science, it is natural science. Any true study of the natural world as it really *is*, will show *abundance* in all things, in all life forms. It is naturally so, for it cannot be any other way. The wind blows. The rain falls. The seed germinates. The animals prosper. New growth prevails. All is well in the world.

Trust that abundance prevails within the eternal nature of God

Negative Expression

To catch a cold is such a normal everyday event that few people ever stop to think about what a cold actually is. What the reality of the situation might be. So, what is it that could be going on here? We would say that a cold happens because it is a natural expression of negative energy within the body.

It is, in fact, an expression of *resistance* to the natural flow of the energy of life all around us. If we fight or push against anything, we are trying to resist that which *is* and attempting to alter the law of cause and effect. In so doing, we become stressed. We weaken our immune system and infection is the result. The normal healthy balance of the body is upset and the more we resist then the more we stress, until distress is the result.

When we resist, we push against the universe and so naturally does the universe push back. And no matter how much energy and effort we might expend, the universe will always match it in equal and opposite measure. So we can say that there is no winner, since both contestants are evenly matched at all times. But there is, indeed, a loser. For eventually our human resources reach their limit and then surrender must follow, sooner or later. It is law. It is Universal law.

When we resist something, it is usually because we have reacted emotionally to that something. It is an interesting observation that when we get a cold, the body naturally raises the core temperature in order to resolve the situation. In like manner does the wire in the electrical circuit get hot. Both are examples of resistance.

Perhaps we might say then that an energy flow is happening. The potential between a positive and a negative emotional position is being equalised and homeostasis will be the end result. We can say that a cold is the expression of a negative energy potential, creating stress upon the body and causing a loss of balance. This loss of equilibrium will eventually cause disease and illness.

We can say also that a positive energy potential creates health and well-being within the body. *We are the expression of our thoughts.* We might say that as an expression of those energies, joy is positive and illness is negative.

Often we react emotionally when we resist. As we try to push back against unwanted circumstance we express that emotion physically, emotionally and mentally. When we go with the natural flow do we feel ourselves positive and when we go against do we feel negative.

At school we learn that this world is made of solid things. That this physical universe works in predictable ways. We learn that there are things to do and places to be. We learn, in fact, about physical energy and so we become *involved* in this physical world of form, which has been made real all about us. And we are reassured and comforted by all these things.

But of what are we ever taught about our feelings? It is a rare thing indeed, for children to be tutored at school in emotional energies. Unlike the world of things, this energy is invisible and we can even become unconscious of our deepest emotional feelings. Few people ever really understand the profound significance of emotion, yet it is something which everyday we all experience.

We can often feel strong emotion as we respond to events around us and if we resist them, so then do we feel stress. Most people are unaware of the hidden consequences of this stress, whereby the normal healthy balance is upset and we then might become ill. Sometimes we are forced to slow down or even give up the fight, allowing then the healing process to begin. When we stop resisting a situation, so do we allow our natural energy to flow once more and a healthy equilibrium is restored within the body. The negative energy potential has been equalised and we then can feel ourselves positively joyful once more.

Health and well-being is the positive expression of life

Positive Expression

Picture yourself, if you will, as a person who has got up late one morning. You have got out of bed on the wrong side today. The alarm clock hasn't gone off and suddenly it's panic stations. There's no hot water and the toast gets burnt. In the rush to get out to the car you leave your purse or wallet behind on the kitchen table.

The car doesn't start straightaway and then when you finally get moving you get stuck in a traffic jam, where normally the roads are clear. You arrive late for work. The boss just happens to be standing by the door as you walk in and he glowers at you.

We have all had a day like that, have we not? A day where nothing seems to go right at all. A day when we seem to be always in the wrong place at the wrong time. We were probably stressed as we fell asleep and then felt stressed again, as we awoke. And so does the day continue to be a stressful one. It seems as though we are swimming against the tide of events. And we are.

In modern life, we so easily forget that we are creators. We have a choice. But we go to work every day swimming mostly upstream, with only the occasional respite. We become used to it and so we expect it. Our senses become dulled. Our life then becomes dulled. And as we react emotionally to these situations, so then do we begin to create more of the same. We seem to be on a treadmill.

It is, however, one of our very own making. Have we not forgotten something important? Indeed, we have. We have forgotten that we are creating our lives. We have forgotten that we have free will and that we do not need to have a bad day. 'What do you mean we have free will!' you say. 'I have to go to work!' you say. We would say that you have forgotten a fundamental truth about yourself.

Let us consider once more the carousel. You have forgotten the *stillness* at the centre of things. You have become so caught up with your life that you cannot seem to switch off and you never stop. Your mind is going round and round and round. Life just goes on, and on, and on.... creation never stops. What then is the answer to this never-ending-merry-go-round?

As soon as you can, take a break. It is very important not to fill this space with activity and things. Fill it instead with *nothing.* Try to be still for a short time. To start with this may be difficult and can feel uncomfortable. So let go of trying. Let go of struggle. Just let go. Become still. Be still. Just *be.*

The answer is to get off that horse on the merry-go-round and find once more your place of stillness. The non-motion at the centre of the carousel. When you stand still at the centre of your thoughts, so then do you become your true self and you find once more your *joy.*

And as you begin to feel that joy again, your days start to improve. You will awaken earlier and feel refreshed, enjoying breakfast and the drive to work. You will arrive early. The boss is so impressed that you will get a promotion. Life will begin to be good again. You will find once more your health. You will find once more your well-being. Your life is now a positive expression of who you are.

More often do you find yourself in the right place at the right time and synchronicity abounds in your life. No longer needing to resist, you find yourself going more with the flow instead. The Universe is now on *your* side, with cause and effect working in *your* favour. You feel more connected and at one with everything. You are more conscious now of who you are and so is your life more full of joy.

Within stillness of being do we find oneness with all life

Respectfulness

In the world today most of the human population lives in urban areas, surrounded constantly by the products of human thought. Few seem to live now within the natural world of Mother Nature. So for them *natural* life has now become *human* life, as created by human thought. And it is naturally so, is it not? For it is with our thoughts that we make our reality.

Many people are now preoccupied with the human reality and have largely forgotten that they too, are a part of Nature. That they still actually *do* live within the wider reality of Mother Earth. Even people who live in the countryside do not really live within Nature any more, for they largely exist within their human reality.

The human race seems to have taken charge of the planet, has it not? It seems to be in control. Human thought can now, apparently, even dominate Mother Nature herself and some people seem to think that they can play around with the genetic coding of *life*.

A life which has been created with great thought and engineered to perfection, slowly over millions of years. We would suggest that they are like little children, playing with wooden building blocks. Trying out different ideas to see what might work. Sometimes the blocks fall over and sometimes they do not. They seem to forget that they are playing with the physical building blocks of *life* itself.

We might say that as little children in play school, they are learning about the law of cause and effect. Now grown up as adults, we would expect them to appreciate that to every action is a reaction. To have learned the lesson that to every thought is a consequence.

The human intellect is a structure of thoughts created by education. Which itself can create other thought forms and structures, with the potential that they can eventually become solid form. Matter. So it matters what we think and what we think matters.

We can say also that human intellect may create thought structures of arrogance and pride. At times, humans can seem to know better than God. But, as we discussed earlier in this text, we *are* God. If therefore, we seem to think that we know better than we already know, then we have probably overstretched ourselves.

As a little child falls over when it tries to take too big a step, so can the human intellect lose its balanced thinking. If we try to walk or run without paying attention to where we are going, then we will trip over something along the way, will we not? Flawed thinking will produce flawed thought forms. And flawed forms will produce flawed matter. It is law. Trial and error is cause and effect in action. Playing with the unknown will create unknown consequences.

Many people now are unaware that they live and have their being within a wider reality. Human creativity is a most marvellous thing. It is, however, still a very pale reflection of the true creativity of the divine presence of God.

Today many forget that they live within *God's Creation*, and that their own creations are but a temporary moment in the eternal ebb and flow of events within the great oceans of existence. They have it would seem become their intellects, and are no longer aware of God. They are a part of God yet they have become apart from God.

The carousel is well designed and creation is perfectly balanced. The motion and non-motion act together in harmony and all is well. The activity of intellect should be balanced by the respect of inner reflection. We would say then, that it is always wise to respect *God's Creation* before our own, and to be thoughtful and respectful of *all* life.

May we learn to trust God and in the stillness of our hearts know wisdom

Thoughtfulness

Picture, if you will, a powerful businessman or woman at the very top of their game as they sit behind their desk with a clear mind and a clear focus. Together with their top aides, all are at the highest level of their professions.

Long term business decisions are made very carefully with much deliberation and forethought. Knowledge gained from experience is combined with that of the present moment to produce well thought out plans for the future of the enterprise. We could say that this is a good example of *thoughtfulness*.

This image, which we now hold within our mind, is very much like the benevolent businesswoman Mother Earth who runs her well managed Establishment wherein new creations are created by the creativity of creative people in well appointed kitchens.

And we can see that there exists a clear vision of the course ahead. Thus is the voyage undertaken and the ship of life steered towards the desired destination. All things being equal, that is to say, all waves of cause and effect being equal and opposite, then the ship will easily make port and the voyage will be successful.

We can say that groups of people in business demonstrate purpose and a clear sense of direction. The World of Business has been built upon a world of material things and is therefore relatively stable. It consists of structures of thought forms which are steadfast in their being. And in like manner has the World of Nature been designed and created. It is steadfast in the being of itself. We can say also that specific groups of plants and animals live with direction and a clear sense of purpose.

Now consider a dictator or politician at the top of their profession. They cling precariously to power trying to stand upright upon the constantly shifting sands of public opinion, steadfastly trying to face the waves of thought coming at them from every direction.

Not knowing which way to turn, they never get a moment of peace from political infighting, international situations and the incessant news media stories. On top of that they have personal concerns and family life which, like the rest of us, they too have to live. So it is no surprise then to find that they never really manage to walk in a straight line, let alone think in one. We could say that this is a good example of *thoughtlessness.*

For there is so little thought actually being thought about so many thoughts. The excesses of economic power is balanced by political power, in like manner to energy flows in nature. Never before, has economic power so easily been able to touch almost every person and corner of the world. Never before, has there been such pressing need for more thoughtfulness in the leaders of the human world.

In ages past, most chiefs of society would put great thought into their decisions. They had the time to think about them and ponder the possible outcomes. They were often people of thoughtfulness, who looked for inspiration from the wise men and women of God.

Whether by design or through fear and superstition, prophets and seers have always been much sought after. For with inner stillness, have they gained access to *God's Wisdom.* Countless generations have asked them for help and placed their problems in God's hands.

Today, we would say that there is a lack of respectfulness towards God and the prophets. People no longer seek help from the Spirit World. The wisdom, knowledge and experience of the ancestors is largely being ignored and instead is the intellect of scientists being used to further economic argument and political statement. With all the great resources at their disposal and with all their thinking, the modern leaders of today have so little thoughtfulness.

**May the wisdom of God be reflected within the stillness
of our minds**

Mindfulness

Imagine yourself, if you will, to be a bird upon the wing. Flying free with wings outstretched. You feel the air as it rushes past your body completely enfolding you. You are feeling very relaxed, but suddenly a gust of wind buffets your little body and you are pushed sideways. You tilt your head slightly and in response your whole body now slides down through the air and you allow yourself to go with the flow of the movement. You decide to turn into the wind and you do so, adjusting your feathers without thinking. Up and up you soar, high up into a deep blue sky. It's so exhilarating and you see other birds flying about you. Your territory is visible far below. You are free. You are you. You are a bird upon the wing.

And now imagine yourself to be a tiger in the bush. You are slowly walking along the path which you have made for yourself, as you patrol the perimeter of your territory. You can feel the soft sweet smelling earth beneath your paws as you pad along silently. Your whiskers gently brush the plants. You hear every sound. Smelling the air you are aware of the animals about you. You are relaxed and comfortable, all is well in your world. You know your surroundings so well. You know every rock, every pool, every tree, every animal. You are free. You are you. You are a tiger in the bush.

And now imagine yourself to be a human being walking in the forest. You are feeling relaxed and you know this territory so well. You know the birds calling out to you from the stand of trees to your left. You know the clear gentle stream flowing with such quiet vigour over to your right. You feel the soft earth and the leaves underfoot, as you walk silently through the green undergrowth. The plants brush your legs softly and you acknowledge their presence as you pass them by. You glance at some shy deer in the clearing, who suddenly look up and then relax again. They know you and you know them. You feel at peace. All is well in your world. You are free. You are you. You are a person walking in the forest.

And now imagine yourself to be a human being walking to work in a busy town. Noisy cars and lorries rush close by as you try to walk quickly along the crowded pavement. The blast of a car horn makes you jump. Overhead a jet aircraft roars loudly as it takes off from a nearby airport. Suddenly, a police car speeds by with sirens and lights blazing away. You get to work and your day is filled with noisy machinery, people talking and music playing loudly over the speaker system. You are not relaxed. You do not feel free. You are not really being you. You are just a person at work in a busy town.

We would say that mindfulness is a quality of mind and that the quality of your mind depends upon that which you put your mind upon for when you put the attention of your mind to anything then do you become mindful of that thing, whatever it may be.

Your quality of mind then is a direct consequence of that which you are focused upon, of that which you are being attentive to, of that which you are being or doing in any particular moment.

You have just been mindful of being a bird on the wing and a tiger in the bush. We might say that your quality of mind is a reflection of the world about you, and in your mind that you are a reflection of your world. You become your world and your world becomes you.

Thoughts and creativity are directed by the quality of your mind, by your mindfulness, by who you are in your world, by who you are being in this moment. So be mindful of yourself and try to be more mindful of others.

So are you mindful of being free and being yourself? We would say that you are *always* free and *always* yourself, no matter what your focus of attention in any given moment.

May we learn to be conscious of who we are in our world

The Silent Pool

We now wish for you to relax and become calm. To be still. To be mindful of these words, as we speak them to you from the pages of this book. Hear our words in your mind as we speak them to you.

We wish to paint for you a picture within your mind, which we have created within our minds. We wish to paint for you a picture, from our minds into your mind.

It is an image of peacefulness and stillness. So if you can try to be peaceful and still, as we pick up our brush and begin to dip the fine quality tip into the pot of ink.

We wish for you to prepare for us a canvas of fine quality paper, pinned to a good wooden frame which is light in weight. The paper is stretched taut, white and pure in colour. Can you see this pristine surface in your mind? Can you feel the smoothness of the paper and smell the fragrance of the wood? It is good.

We are now ready to begin. We wish for you to relax, so that you are able to receive the picture we wish to give to you with ease and clarity. The ink is now upon the brush, waiting for us to move our hand across the paper with swift strokes of the pen.

Be still, and you will become aware of these brush strokes as they gradually begin to build up the picture before your eyes. Slowly, the details are taking shape now upon the white surface in front of you.

First you see a tree. As the shape fills in, you see that it is perfectly formed and well balanced. It is a lovely tree. It is not too tall or short, not too big or small. It is just right and perfect in every way. You feel moved by the great beauty of this tree and it truly is a most wonderful sight to behold.

Next, you notice that there is something below this tree and you become aware that you are looking at a large pool of water. There is no wind blowing at all and the surface of this deep clear pool is perfectly still and calm. Everything is very still, absolutely still. There is no movement or sound in this picture.

You marvel at the simplicity of our brush strokes, as we paint this picture for you. We pause not as we masterfully move our hand, controlling the fine quality brush as it moves deftly across the surface of the paper.

You see now a tree which is perfect in every way, standing beside a deep pool of crystal clear water. All is peaceful and all is calm. All is quiet.

The only sound you hear is that of the brush as it works tirelessly at its given task. It is fulfilling its reason for being and allowing us to paint this picture for you, as we speak these words upon this page. You marvel at the simplicity and the beauty of it all.

We now ask of you to imagine yourself to be sitting beside this pool. Can you smell the dampness of the water and the refreshing coolness of the air? Can you smell the delicate perfume coming from the beautiful flowers upon the tree? All is silent and calm. Everything is perfectly still.

The brush is moving very quickly and before your eyes you see now a figure beginning to take shape, sitting by the side of the pool. Someone is sitting upon a grassy bank and staring intently at the surface of the water. You seem to recognise the features of this individual and feel that you know them.

This person is very familiar to you. You can see that they are wearing fine quality clothes and the folds of beautiful soft material fall gently about them in perfect symmetry.

They sit perfectly still, looking directly at the surface of the water. You are feeling relaxed. All is well and you feel comfortable with the idea that you know this person.

As you look at this eloquent picture before you, with the delicate brush strokes of ink placed so precisely upon the pure white surface of the paper, so do you begin to slowly become aware that you are now looking through the eyes of this person, who is sitting beside the pool.

You can see the body of water stretching out before you and it is crystal clear and still. You can see light sparkling upon the surface of this water, reflecting back to you. You can see the tree standing there in all its majestic beauty, perfectly formed.

You feel calm. You breathe in and hold your breath for a moment. You have now become perfectly still. You are now absolutely still.

In the eternal moment, you see the pure reflection of the tree perfectly formed upon the surface of the water.

As if the reflection of the tree is as solid and real as is the tree itself. There is no distortion.
You have perfectly clear vision.

Within that stillness you see a perfect reflection of reality mirrored upon the surface of your mind.

All waves of cause and effect are in perfect balance.
There is complete stillness within your mind.
Thoughts and emotions no longer exist.

Your mind is a perfect mirror.
You have clear vision.

Crystal clear.
Clarity of vision.

You breathe in and out in a perfect rhythm.
You are feeling relaxed.
You are peaceful.
All is well.

We have just painted the picture of a *Spiritual Master*.
Someone who is master of their Spirit.

Complete stillness within and complete stillness without,
master of their self.

Allowing clear perception of reality to be reflected within the mind.

Inner and outer reflection are one
In perfect vision.

May you see perfect beauty in your life

Meditation

Spiritual teachers down the ages have always taught of the great virtue to be found in *meditation* and the practise thereof. Many techniques have been created and developed down the millennia, for the spiritual student to find and eventually attain to a calmness of mind, thus allowing them to both observe themselves and the life around them. To allow them to stand at the centre of their thoughts.

In essence the teaching is often very simple. However, as you may already have discovered even the simplest of instructions can be almost impossible to complete. To the beginner new to spiritual practice, the art of meditation will seem at first to be unattainable. Indeed the simplicity itself of the command to be still is often the biggest obstacle to progress at the start. Be warned, my friend, that great diligence will be required to attain knowledge of the art of meditation.

Book after book and essay after essay has been written upon this subject, expounding the various and multitudinous techniques to be found in the study of this very serious matter of spiritual discipline. Much effort and concentration will be expended in the search for knowledge. The new scholar will soon become lost in a great ocean of thoughts which wash over them like the waves of the sea upon a beach. Occasionally, perhaps a small pebble may be washed up and cause you to stub a toe painfully, as you walk along the soft sands gazing out with a yearning desire towards the distant and boundless infinitely vast oceans of existence.

We would say that the first requirement of any new student is to learn the art of discrimination. To look with a discerning eye upon the information available and distinguish between that which is useful and that which is not. To the outsider this might seem to be a simple enough affair, but to the student of spiritual matters rarely does a straightforward situation turn out to be anything but straight.

The twists and turns of the path can be confusing and bewildering, teaching the student to keep a clear mind and to maintain a good sense of direction. As you may already know, we must each tread our own path of truth towards the *Holy Mountain of Enlightenment*. The directions given to another will be perfect for them but may not be so useful for you to follow. You might find yourself wandering aimlessly, hopelessly lost in a great wilderness of ever expanding knowledge

A wise teacher would always say that should you ever lose your way, then stand still and take fresh bearings in order to find your new position. Hold up your inner compass to the light of the Sun and you will be shown the best way forward. You will always be guided along the Way, as long as you continue to hold a vision of where you are going. The *Light* shineth forever in the darkness for those who looketh up to Heaven and see the *Glory*.

So if you are new to meditation my friend, are you now ready to pick up the gauntlet of challenge and ride out into the tournament? Once you start there is no going back for you can only ever go forwards. So hold onto the reins, grip your saddle tight with your knees and keep your balance.

We wish to teach to you a very simple method of meditation, an old school of thought dating back many thousands of years. Go outside and find for yourself a little flower sitting in the shade and join with this little one. Sit there quietly, as it waits patiently for the sun to come up. Eventually is the tiny flower enlightened and then does it open itself up to the warmth and the light. It does so willingly and without struggle. It surrenders to *God's Love*. All you need to do is to follow the wisdom of the tiny flower and open up your heart towards the *Light of God*.

May we open to the love of God and find enlightenment

Inspiration

Do you live in or near to a city or town with a ring road? Have you ever experienced driving or being driven around just such a road, going somewhere and getting nowhere fast? Sometimes does your life seem to be nothing more than a big ring road? Around which you drive your car, sitting behind the wheel and watching all those familiar landmarks pass you by again and again? If so, perhaps you are in need of some inspiration.

Our friend, who is writing this book for you, has often felt like this in his life. Desperate to get away from everyday routine and break free from the never-ending-traffic-jam which is the modern urban lifestyle. Round and round did he drive. Sometimes literally did he manifest this vision of his life, finding himself driving on the M25 Orbital Motorway around London. This has often been described, with good reason, as the largest car park in Britain. Whether for just a few moments or a few hours a motor vehicle when stationary is parked, is it not? Do you feel sometimes that your life is not on the move? If so, then perhaps you are in need of some inspiration.

Sometimes, our friend would become so frustrated with his life that he needed change. So he swapped the day job for shift work. The new routine was at first a welcome change but the relief was short lived. From long experience he knew that working shifts is very tiring and unhealthy, so he changed back to a day job. It is as if he had pulled off at a junction on the M25, driving over the flyover to the next roundabout and taking the exit leading back down onto the ring road. But this time going in the opposite direction. As we have previously discussed there are no opposites in this physical world, only relative positions. So our friend was driving first clockwise and then anti-clockwise, whilst still going around the same ring road of life. Things change but stay the same. Has your life been like this? If so, then perhaps you are in need of some inspiration.

All is well with the world as you drive freely at speed along the open road, when suddenly up ahead you spot those red tail lights going on. Your heart sinks and soon your life comes to a sudden standstill. Has your life sometimes seemed to be like this? If so, then perhaps you are in need of some inspiration.

Traffic is flowing quickly and smoothly when all of a sudden everything slows down dramatically. Everyone keeps moving but progress is painfully slow. There does not seem to be any reason for it, until eventually you spot an incident on the other side of the road. The delay has been caused by the other drivers slowing down to look at what is going on. Does life sometimes frustrate you when progress is slow? If so, then inspiration may be just what you need.

We might say that to be inspired is to get an idea. The image of a light bulb turning on inside someone's head has now come vividly to mind. Illumination then, is the key. Often, do we not find that a source of inspiration has been there right in front of us all the time? We just simply did not see it. We did not recognise it.

We might say that the meaning of inspire is to breathe new life into someone or something. To feel *alive*, once again! That inspiration we sometimes seek is on open display, for road signs large and small alert us as we approach a turning upon the highways of life.

Learn to read the *signs.* You may get some *inspiration* as you drive along the M25 and spot the *sign* for the M3. Suddenly, you may see a *vision* of Bournemouth and the New Forest, and so off you go in that direction. If not prepared, plan ahead for the next opportunity and you will then be ready to go off and find a new adventure.

Life is an eternal merry-go-round of new experiences to enjoy

Perception

Have you ever been out shopping and searched for something but could not find it? You may or may not have been in a rush. You looked and looked, but as hard as you looked you just could not seem to find that elusive item.

Up and down and round and round you go, until you stand still completely exasperated. You decide to ask the shop assistant who is standing right in front of you, to direct you towards the product. Smiling brightly they then promptly turn round on the spot. They reach for the shelf and suddenly there it is, in their hand! You feel slightly embarrassed and you wonder how on earth you could have missed it, for there it was right in front of you.

Yet you saw it not. How can this be? 'I could not see it for looking!' you say. 'My head must have been somewhere else!' you say. And we say no, it was not. Your head was in the shop all the time. You were totally focused upon finding the item and yet you found it not.

We would agree it is a strange thing, indeed. We seem to be living in a physical world and yet sometimes with our physical vision, do we see not. Truly, it is a most peculiar happenance. So you might think that it is a type of magic perhaps, an illusion. But we would say most emphatically that magic is definitely *not* an illusion. There has been much confusion caused by the fact that stage illusionists describe themselves as 'magicians', because what you see is not what you get.

We would say that *magic* is real and that it is the illusion of trickery which is not so real. It is the so-called 'magicians' who are the real charlatans and tricksters, because they appear to make something happen which does not. A *true magician* makes something happen. We must say, however, that the illusion itself is real. For it happens, does it not? But whether you can actually see it or not is another matter, of course.

'We all live in the real world!' you say. 'What you see is what you get!' you say. And we would agree, it's true. It is a fact that real life is not an illusion, so no trickery here then. The chair you sit upon is real, is it not? The floor you stand upon is real, is it not? The item on your shopping list is real, is it not? Yet still you did not see it.

Maybe the fake 'magicians' have something to tell us. Maybe they are trying to show us something and somehow we just fail to see it. Maybe they are trying to show us that not everything we see is real. Perhaps everything is not what it appears to be. That is to say, our *reality* is not all that it seems to be. That which we sometimes think to be, not always *is*. For the lost and invisible item was in the shop all the time, and so sometimes then we just do not get what we see. So is life *real*? Or is it all just an illusion?

We would say that when we realise something, so then do we make it real and when we make something real, then so do we realise it. With our thoughts do we make our world. Thought becomes form and form becomes matter. And you must agree that the chair you sit upon is a very important matter indeed, for without it you would fall to the floor with a bump!

So there you are, looking for the item in the shop and you think the thought that it seems to be invisible. And so it *is*. As if you have waved a magic wand, the item is now lost to your sight and because you cannot see it, so then does it become lost to you. You think it lost and it becomes so. And so it *is*.

'My mind must be playing tricks with me!' you say. And yes, we agree. For truly, is it *all* in your mind. But whether you can actually see it or not, now that *is* the question. To perceive is to be aware, to be conscious of.... and how *perceptive* are you, my friend?

We pray you find that which you are looking for

Visualisation

So what you are trying to tell me then is that what I see is what I get and what I get is what I see. Well, to be honest with you, I just can't see it myself. I can't really see what you're getting at.

We might say that the reason why you cannot see it is very clear indeed to us but not to yourself, of course. That is because the image of what we are saying to you is within our minds, but not in your mind. So we would say that you cannot *see* it simply because you cannot bring it to mind. Your mind that is, since we ourselves are very mindful of that which we wish to say to you.

It is always a good idea to try to keep a clarity of mind at all times. To always keep a clear head about you. Therefore, with this in mind we shall give to you a very simple example of a *visualisation*. So simple that you will be amazed, astounded in fact. Your face will make such a picture that we wish only that you were able to see it. So, my friend, can you see yet where we are going with all of this? Are you ready to perceive your *insight* yet?

Think of an apple. A nice ripe and rosy juicy apple. Hold on to this thought in your mind, hold it, hold it. Keep on holding on to it and eventually, sooner or later, you will find that you hold in your hand that apple. It may be in a few seconds or minutes, hours or days, weeks or months or perhaps even years. Time is never a problem for we live in eternity, do we not? But we can say that the stronger the vision you hold of that apple, then the more will that apple you shall hold represent that vision. Doubt not. If you hold the thought of that apple, it will eventually appear in your hand. It is law.

Let us say that you have this apple now. But if you have not one ready to hand, then please feel free to use your imagination instead. This is, after all, an exercise in visualisation. Roll it in your fingers and feel the texture and solidity. Hold it up to your nose and smell the fragrance. Bite into it and taste the fullness of the flavour.

Chew it and then swallow it. You have just *realised* the image of that apple, which earlier you saw within your mind's eye. You have made it *real* with your thoughts. It is a thought form. It is a thought made form. You have just been eating a visualisation of the apple and it matters not whether that apple is an imaginary one held in your mind, or a more solid reality held in your hand.

For it is the *idea* of the apple which has become more real to you. And if you are indeed holding an apple at this very moment, what you are experiencing is the physical representation of that idea. As a matter of fact, you are holding a form of the thought of that apple. An experience of the *visualisation* in the physical sense.

Well, my friend. How simple is that? What you see is what you get. Are you beginning to see what we are saying, at last? What you see is the image in your mind's eye and that is exactly what you get.

We can say that when an illusionist pulls a white rabbit out of an empty hat, that is what you see. That is your reality and it is not a trick to you. It is real. The visualisation within your mind of the trick is real and so it becomes your reality. The white rabbit truly is pulled from an empty hat. We might say then that although your reality is an illusion, it is nevertheless a real one.

Did you like that? We pulled a neat little trick on you there. A little magical trick, we might say. For when we *visualise*, so do we make things real. We make it happen. It truly is magical, it's pure magic.

Remember, a true magician is someone who makes things happen. Visualisation then is pure wizardry, if you had but the wit to see it! We would say that a wizard is a wise sage. A philosopher skilled in the magical art of visualisation, *a true magician.*

Verily do I say unto thee that thou art the apple of my eye

In The Picture

When did you last look at a picture? We do not mean just a casual glance, we mean *looked*. Really looked hard. What did you see? On the face of it maybe you saw canvas or paper, pastel or pencil, paint or ink. And perhaps you saw a hanging frame of some kind.

But what else did you see? Although you did indeed look at the picture itself, you did not really take much notice of it. We would suggest that you were actually looking at the picture of the picture.

And what did you see? You might well answer that you did, in fact, see the picture. But did you? What did you really see? So yes, you looked at the picture but what did you *actually* see? Are you getting the picture yet, of where we are going to go with all this?

Yes, visually and in your reality did you see the picture. And so no argument there then, no tricks here. But if you think about it, you might agree that you were not necessarily paying much attention to the actual picture itself.

What did you *really* see? We would say that you were seeing the picture within your mind. That you created a mindful visualisation of the physical representation before your eyes. Although you were using your physical vision to view the physical picture, in truth however were you seeing it within your mind's eye. The reality all around us is reflected within our minds, is it not?

Think about what that means, for a moment. We are saying that you *look* at a picture with your eyes but *see* it with your mind. We might say then that looking and seeing are not the same thing. That to look is to observe but to see is to create a vision.

Consider once more the carousel. We observe when we stand at the centre of our thoughts and we create when we use our thoughts. Thus we both observe and create experience simultaneously.

So, are you in the picture yet? Have we *in-formed* you as to what is really going on here? Can you see it? Perhaps you are still only observing the facts of the matter and maybe your head is spinning round again, like the carousel. If so, maybe we should take a break. Be still a moment and observe once more the situation. Perhaps we should examine a picture itself, in more detail.

Imagine, if you will, an oil painting of a landscape before you. It hangs upon the wall in a huge, most magnificently carved frame of gilded oak. The picture is large with many square yards of canvas covered in bright swathes of colour. Bold brush strokes detail the scenes with alacrity. Truly a wonderful sight to behold, it is so big that you have to stand back to view it clearly, as you try to take it all in. And what do you see?

Trees, bushes, flowers, grass, birds, blue sky and clouds. Sunlight perhaps, with light and shadow. Animals, fields, fences, hedgerows, gates, tree blossom perhaps or autumn leaves. A river, a lake or a pond. A mansion, a cottage or a barn. A church, a village or a town. People perhaps, with vehicles, boats or aircraft. And maybe there are some hills or mountains in the background.

Are you getting the picture *now*? Images, which the artist once held in mind, have been translated onto the canvas in paint. The painter has visualised the picture and created a mental image. This has then been successfully re-created upon the blank canvas.

So we might say then that you are seeing the thoughts of the artist. Not just with your own eyes but also with your own thoughts, for you create within your own mind the thought forms that you see. The reality of the artist has been realised and made form and you have then created a reflection within your own mind of that reality. *This is the picture that you see.*

We create yet also are we created within the loving mind of God

A Photograph

It has been written that a picture is worth a thousand words and we would agree. Indeed, the oil painting described as above would probably need at least a whole book or more perhaps, to contain all of the words which might be associated with it. How can this be so?

You may well ask, as to why it should be that an ordinary picture can visually represent such a great multitude of words, such a vast literary compendium of commentary and description. A clue to the answer here, perhaps, may lie with just one single word, *represent*. For the painting represents the details it contains, does it not? And those details themselves can, in turn, be a representation of ideas and facts. And these again can be represented by words.

Consider, if you will, a photographic picture of the famous railway locomotive the *Flying Scotsman*, as it steams steadily across the Ribblehead Viaduct in North Yorkshire. It is summer and the sun is shining in a deep blue sky. The fells are a wonderful, luxuriously rich green backdrop to the majestic scene.

The neat lines of this beautiful steam engine are supremely eloquent and the splendid engineering is of the highest possible standard. Smoke billows voluminously as it thunders along the track pulling a line of carriages.

Maybe you are enjoying the countryside with it's fine rolling fells, drystone walls and the occasional stone barn scattered about here and there. You can just make out the small families of sheep as they go about their day on the open hillsides.

You admire the fine engineering of the stone viaduct as it sweeps across the valley, arching over the sparkling blue waters of the river Ribble. The train really does look grand in this glorious setting. Or perhaps you are a railway enthusiast and you are picturing yourself sitting at the controls and driving this enormous engine.

You smell the smoke and the steam and you feel the heat from the firebox as the fireman stokes the boiler. You feel the wind in your hair as this powerhouse of mechanical excellence roars along the tracks. With sheer joy you pull the whistle and a huge smile lights up your face. What a most wonderful engine this is, you think to yourself.

Maybe you are an historian instead and to you this magnificent machine represents the pinnacle of steam locomotive engineering in Britain. The fine lines and superbly engineered design are the result of more than 100 years of continuous development, often at the leading edge of technology. Great Britain led in the creation of the railways and built the world's first national network of lines. Then engineers went on to build many of the great railways of the world.

It would require many libraries of books to hold all of the words written or spoken about this one photograph. Each observer sees a unique internal perspective known only to them and both subjective and objective points of view are perceived. So many thoughts and emotions will be inspired, and *all* of them from *one* single picture. It is truly remarkable, is it not? But there is yet more, for the picture captures a moment in *Space-Time*. It is a recording, if you like, of a particular moment when various activities were happening in the reality of this Universe.

If you were sensitive enough, then you might just become aware of the waiter serving a young man in the dining car. The lady taking a photo out of the window in the third carriage or the frail elderly gentleman celebrating his wedding anniversary with his wife. Even of a tropical storm deep in the pacific ocean and a volcano going off in Hawaii. You might even become aware of the star many light years away from Earth, which is exploding. All this *reality* has been captured in the moment of this *one* photograph.

With love may you reach out to touch the whole Universe

Simplicity

The more we look, the more do we see. The more we feel, the more are we emotional. The more we think, the more busy our mind. We all live today in a world so busy with thoughts, here and there and everywhere. It is a world crammed absolutely full of the energy of thoughts, whether human or otherwise. Everywhere then are we surrounded by activity and motion, by things done or to be done. Everywhere are we surrounded by thought forms made real and the symbols thereof. Everywhere, are we surrounded by *thoughts*.

Truly, is the human world such a *busy* world of thinking and doing. It is an enormous ever-growing whirlpool of energy, swirling round continuously and sometimes it can literally put us into a spin. In the psychic sense, mental sense, emotional sense and even in a physical sense. It is as if the carousel is spinning round ever faster and we are sometimes having to hang on, and grip tightly for dear life.

We live within an environment of energy, movement and thought. We live within an atmosphere of emotional energy. We live within an atmosphere of mental energy. If you were but to stop awhile and reflect upon this reality, you might be amazed by what you will discover. The truth which shall be shown to you, mirrored within your mind, will surprise you. For you are living in a human society and are overwhelmed daily by very strong *active* thought forms, all trying to get your attention, your focus and your mind space.

The television channels with their programmes and their news bulletins. The radio stations which transmit for twenty four hours non-stop, day in and day out. The newspapers, the magazines and the books. The advertisements everywhere trying so hard to pull you into their vision of expectation. The signs which surround you in the supermarket always exhorting you to buy, buy, buy. The shop assistant needing you to buy something to boost their commission. The second-hand-car-salesman who is trying to sell you a wreck.

As you walk down the high street or shopping mall think of all the shop keepers who are struggling to make ends meet, who cry out desperately within their minds and hearts for customers to call in. Think too of the successful business owners who also cry out for more customers with all their hearts and minds, that they might become ever more prosperous.

So are we bombarded every day by these multitudinous energetic thoughts, which reach out to us and can often affect our minds and our thinking. We would suggest that you learn to observe yourself as you go about daily life. And so become more conscious of your thoughts and of how you are thinking. Gradually, so will you begin to perceive when your mind is being influenced.

Thus you become more aware of those outside thoughts which have crept into your thinking processes. You will resist the big shop sign, *'an offer you cannot refuse'* to buy two dozen chocolate gateaux for the price of a dozen, when you need only a single cake.

We should remember that our minds will reflect the world around us and if that reality is in a tumult, so then shall our minds be also. Our thoughts will race round hither and thither until there seems to be no end to it. Think then of the carousel and get off the horse.

Take a break, in any way that you can. Still your mind and calm the choppy *Seas of Your Thought*. Try to find once more your mental balance by focusing upon the distant horizon. Find your sea legs and you will not dizzy and fall. Find *simplicity* of mind and so shall you keep your *own* mind.... mind you, this really is not so easy to accomplish in this mental world of today.

(The poem If, by Rudyard Kipling)

If you can keep your head when all about you are losing theirs

Protection

So my friend, try if you can to always maintain a clear head and be joyful and be calm. Think your *own* thoughts. Keep your *own* mind. Live your *own* life and just be yourself. And then so shall ye be in no need of protection. For truly can we say unto thee, if thou be arrayed in the armour of God, so then will ye be forever safe and secure within the loving embrace of the Divine.

We would suggest that if you think you are in need of protection, then shall it be and it will be so. We shall be discussing the concept of protection in more detail in Book Two of this series of books. We can say, however, that a person who is joyful shall live a life of joy and a person who is fearful shall live a life of fear. How you live your life will depend entirely upon how you are feeling, in any given moment.

So we might say then that we should be afraid of the fear of having the idea of being fearful. But what *is* there in life, to be afraid of? Indeed naught but the very *idea* of fear itself. Whence comes this fear? Is it imagination or is it real? How has the idea come to mind?

Consider the news bulletins which continuously bombard you every day with information about the bad and unfortunate experiences of other people. Alas, truly does their misfortune become yours as you reflect their reality within your own mind.

As you believe it and make it so, do you then begin to incorporate *their* reality into your *own*. You begin to create new thought form structures within your mind. And the more that you think about it, then the more does it become into your reality.

And so gradually do you begin to live in fear. A fear of this and a fear of that, a fear of that and a fear of this. For you have educated your intellect in realities which you do *not* wish to experience.

And so do you now begin to *resist* the natural energy flow of the life around you. Your fear of being outside keeps you shut within and your fear of being shut within keeps you outside. Your fear of heights keeps you on the ground. Your fear of a motor accident keeps you off the roads. Your fear of being struck by lightning keeps you away from trees. And so on and so forth....

Slowly, does your existence become more and more stressed. Your lack of ease eventually becomes disease. It is as if your fear helps you to create the very situations which you do not want to happen. And your intellect will justify said happenings, that same intellect which watched the news bulletins in the first place. So your fear is justified to you and is now your reality. You are *realising* the fear.

In truth, does it exist only because you make it so. For you have put your focus of attention upon the very things which you do not wish for to happen and so do they happen. From just a simple idea at the beginning, have you created complicated thought structures within your mind. The initial idea has been embellished by more thought, until you have a mental structure. As you then begin to experience those thoughts in your life, so do you react with emotion and thus you create still yet *more* thought forms.

Think it and it is so. Therefore verily do we say unto thee, with *joy* in your heart will you bring *joy* into your life. Be not fearful, for thou art of God. When thou knowest this within thine own heart, so shalt thou know *Divine Love*. This moment if thou art fearful, look up to the *Light*. Ask for help and it shall be given unto thee. With love in thy heart, truly wilt thou be wearing the armour of God and thou shalt know not fear.

Love with all thy heart, with all thy mind and with all thy soul and thou shalt know God

Heal Thyself

We shall discuss the subject of *healing* in more depth in Book Two of this series. For the moment, however, let us now look at the most basic concept which lies behind all healing. Think it and it is so.

Thus if you think of yourself as healthy, then *healthy* shall ye be. We can say also that if you think yourself an unhealthy person, then *unhealthy* shall ye be. Remember, that you create your reality with your thoughts. So my friend, do you think well or ill of yourself?

The first requirement of anyone who desires to be of good health is to think *only* in terms of well-being. And so then will they hold that vision of themselves and as they do, so will they feel it and then the more that they feel their well-being, so shall they live it. The reality within your mind shall reflect back to you and it will be so.

Consider how you felt when you lived as a very young child. Did you think then in terms of being healthy or unhealthy? No, you did not. For most children, this is not an issue. They live very much in the moment and if they do knock themselves, feeling hurt and pain, it is often short lived and very quickly do their minds turn towards their next adventure. They pay little attention to the injury and so does it heal itself speedily. Most younger children normally harbour not thoughts of illness and disability but instead hold the vision of a natural sense of well-being, and so it *is*.

Consider how you feel while you live as an adult. You now think in terms of being healthy or unhealthy, do you not? Yes, you do. And it has now become an issue for you. Most adults find it difficult to live consciously within the moment and so then if they do knock themselves, feeling hurt and pain, it is often long lived and very quickly do they turn their minds to the injury. They give it a great deal of attention and so does it heal itself tardily. Most older adults normally harbour not thoughts of natural well-being but instead hold the vision of illness and disability, and so it *is*.

'But that's not true!' you say. 'I caught a virus and it has made me feel ill!' you say. 'Disease is a physical reality!' you say. Yes, it is. And we agree that it is so. However, we are looking and thinking about the *cause* and not the effect. What is it that are you looking and thinking about? Most people in human society are taught to look only at the *effect*, and not from whence it comes.

What then can be done to help resolve imbalance within the body, once normal equilibrium has been altered and natural homeostasis has been lost. As that large ball set rolling downhill begins to gather speed, what can we do about it? If it has been rolling for some time then it will have built up a great deal of momentum. How can we stop it? How can we alter the course of events which have been set in motion? How can we change the e-motion of it all?

The first requirement for anyone who is ill is to remember that you are a creator, you have choice in the matter. You can *change* what is happening in the moment. We would suggest to you that as well as a doctor, you find for yourself a *healer*. You will know when you have met the right person and as you begin to feel benefit from the healing sessions, so shall you begin to turn your mind once more towards a natural feeling of health and a sense of well-being.

With your hands placed firmly upon the wheel once again will you be steering your ship of life onto a new heading, a course which will take you to a new destination. Remember always, that you are an eternal being sailing the vast and endless oceans of existence.

When people heal themselves of illness or injury, then in essence do they change their *reality*. A reality which we shall be discussing in more detail in Book Two of this series. A reality which exists now, in this moment. If you feel not ease then so shall you feel dis-ease. It is as simple as that.

Know within your heart that all is well

The Tug of War

If ye feel not ease, so then shall ye feel dis-ease. Wherefore then doth come this feeling of lack of ease? Does it come from within or without? Is it real or imaginary? Do we react to a situation with stress because of that particular circumstance? Or maybe it is more to do with how we are feeling, how we are relating in the emotional sense to said circumstance. Now to every question is there answer. It is law. It is a cause and an effect.

We would say that the first requirement to finding an answer to this most vexing of questions, is to relax. To be easy about it all. Allow then the answer to come to you, instead of you going out to search high and low for it. Be still. Reflect that stillness deep within your mind. And then shall you perceive the answer, as it shows itself to you within the clearness of your perception with crystal clarity.
So then, be mindful of your awareness.

How are you feeling? Do you feel calm? Do you feel peaceful? Are you aware of contentedness? If so, then perhaps that might be your answer. To *be content*. You feel no anxiety when you are content but instead do you feel easy about yourself and your life. Yes, you may indeed feel physical stress about the body when you undertake activity, especially any strenuous exercise, but otherwise you feel happy and content with your life.

Now that you have *felt* the answer to the question asked, you can begin to understand more clearly the problem. You can be content without doing anything, can you not? Contentedness then is an inner feeling not dependant upon outer activity although you can, of course, feel happy when doing something you enjoy. And so like the piece of wood with two ends, if being content is an inner feeling then so must being stressed be also, for they are relative opposites. And we could say that the pressure and stress which we seem to experience as a single phenomena is, in fact, perceived upon more than one level.

We could say then that perhaps there are two different types of stress, inner and outer. The *physical* experience and the *feeling* experience. If we but stop and reflect awhile, then shall we see that the inner stress is felt upon more than one level. For we feel both emotional and mental tensions, do we not? So we would say then that stress is a multi-dimensional event happening simultaneously across many different levels of our reality and life experience.

My Word! No wonder then that anxiety, something which we all have to live with, is so difficult to try to understand and to resolve. What a big headache it is. No surprise therefore that so many of us fall ill with the worry of it all. For it is indeed a very stressful thing to feel stressed about being stressed about stressful circumstance.

We may feel a clash sometimes between our inner and our outer experiences. At a funeral, perhaps, where we might ourselves be feeling peaceful within yet are we with people who are upset and sad. Also sometimes, perhaps, when we are forced to do something which we do not like. At times, we may even need to undertake an abhorrent activity which pushes us to the limit on all levels.

We can also feel pressure when we are in two minds and just cannot decide the best option. We feel like the handkerchief tied to a rope, being pulled in a tug-of-war. First one way and then the other. The tension is enormous and sometimes we break under the strain. Our instinct pulls us one way and circumstance appears to pull us the other. Perhaps the greatest stress we can suffer is this tug-of-war between the *inner* and *outer* experience. Between observer and observed. Between the stillness at the centre of the carousel and the ever-moving-merry-go-round-of-life.

**Peace be unto thee that ye might feel restful
within a restless world**

The Washing Machine

It would seem then that you live within an *inner world* which has different levels of reality. Well yes, truly are we being on the level with you here. But which level? We can safely say that there is no need to worry too much or become stressed about what it all might mean, for you live it anyway. Your inner experience exists upon more than one plane. You instinctively know this to be a truth, even if you do not put much thought into this matter. And indeed, we might say also that your thoughts often have a mind of their own which reflects upon your reality, whether you know it to be or not.

It would seem too that you live within an *outer world* of things at the same time. A constant and solid reality which is, on the face of it, fairly straightforward in nature. It *is* what it *is*. A tree is a tree. A house is a house. A cat is a cat which is being chased perhaps by a dog which is a dog.

You take comfort and solace in the facts of this fact. Real life is a matter of fact, is it not? So let that be an end to it then. Well that is relatively speaking, of course. What really matters, however, is that this is a matter of some substance. In fact, the substance of reality. The substance of the world you live in. You are indeed yourself a person of considerable substance, whether you believe it to be so or not. For you have a most substantial body, a tangible corporeality which you can even put your finger upon.

But is it all that it seems to be? Is all this substance around you really real? Is it as solid an actuality as you assume it to be? You may already know that scientists think matter is not solid at all, but instead exists almost entirely of empty space. We have to say here, however, that we ourselves can see right through their theories. We would say, most emphatically, that there is definitely much more to all this reality than the *nothing* of empty space. You might need to think about all this, so clear your mind and empty it of all thought. Thus may you be able to contemplate the emptiness of your reality.

We might say that the first requirement to understanding this matter is to clean up your mind. So take your thoughts and put them into a washing machine. Give them a thorough wash and rinse, flushing away down the brain drain the detritus of detail and the stains of education. You will be left with a mind full of clean pure thoughts, now refreshed and full of colour. You will have had a brainwash.

And now just look at something, anything of substance will do. For example, a washing machine. We might also recommend a kettle, watch it boil or perhaps paint, watch it dry. Look at it. Just keep on looking at it and if you *look* for long enough then will you *see* right through it to the truth contained therein.

Consider the matter of your washing machine. At first sight there seems to be not much more to it really, it *is* what it *is*. But have you ever thought about the factory where it was made? All those people who have physically touched this very machine? Think of all the people *involved* in some way with the creation of it. Think about all the assemblers, the draughtsmen, the designers, the managers and also, most importantly, the people working away in the canteen.

Think about everyone *involved* in the manufacture and supply of the raw materials and also the retail business which sold it to you. Think of all the emotions and thoughts which have directly touched this very machine, as all those people went about their day.

Clearly, is there much more *thought* behind this material world than perhaps you might first have thought. For many layers of conscious energy are part of the reality of the washing machine. Likewise, you are not the simpleton you may have thought yourself to be. You are instead a multi-dimensional being living within multi-dimensional reality happening right now in a multi-dimensional existence.

Within the emptiness of your mind is the fullness of your reality

Your Sense of Reality

'But how on earth are we to be able to make any sense whatsoever of all this?' you say. We would say that you are *already* making a *sense* of it. That is what your sense of sense is for, is it not? To make sense of your reality.

If you but stop a moment to think about it, you might just begin to realise that it *all* makes perfect sense. After all, it is a perfectly sensible reality, is it not? There is nothing to be anxious about at all really, nothing to be nervous about. Just be sensible. Great minds have been at work, for what seems like an eternity, to ensure that you have nothing to worry about. So be at peace, my friend.

We would say that it makes perfect sense that nothing makes sense. For most of the reality in this universe is formless thought. It is not so much a reality of things as a reality of no things, *nothing*. And we can say that the formless world of thought is but a nonsense really, a non-sense to the human being living in the world of form.

Now must we use some common sense. For it is plainly a nonsense to imagine that the physical senses of form can perceive something which has *no form*. To do so would be to lose our sense of sanity, would it not? To lose our sense of reality. Our *solid* reality, that is. The world of solid matter. But, as we already know, it turns out that this world of solid things is nothing but empty space.

Is your head spinning yet? Well, it should be. Because this is all so very confusing, in the physical sense. But why should this be so? Because, my friend, how can the physical faculties of perception make anything of something which is *not* physical? For they are designed only to make any real sense of the world of form.

The world of formless thought is just nothing and to the physical body, it simply does not exist. Scientists have found to their great surprise that much of the matter in this universe is nothing. The formless reality of *nothing*.

Your physical senses are part of your physical body and they have form. Your eyes see, your tongue tastes, your nose smells, your skin feels and your ears hear. They connect to the world of form, that is to say, the world of things. And they have *formed* themselves very slowly through the gradual evolution not just of *your* body, but the bodies of *all of life* itself. The formulation of this bodily sense has been consciously developed over many millions of years.

Truly divine is the inspiration behind all of life. We are, in fact, *all* godly creatures. From the single cell of the simple amoeba, to the complicated life forms with which we are familiar in our daily lives. It is of no matter whether your intellect believes it or not, but great minds have thought great thought and we are *all* the living consequence of such. Truly, with *their* thought has *our* reality been created. We live within the *grace* of divine thought.

Now, there *is* a thought! Is all this beginning to make some *sense* to you, at last? If not, then perhaps you need to make use of more than just your normal sense of things. Maybe you also need use of your psychic sense. It operates in a similar fashion to the physical sense but connects not to the world of form. Instead does it relate to the world of the formless, that is to say, the world of thought.

It makes perfect sense then that you should use your *psychic sense* to understand and to realise the invisible world of thoughts, within which you really live. Thoughts that are affecting your everyday reality much more than you might think. The visible world of form is not separated at all from this unseen world of formless energy. Instead is it all connected and linked together within the energy flow and movement of Creation itself, in the creative energy of the *Divine Presence*, within which each one of us lives and has our very being.

To understand something so must we make sense of it

Etheric Body

So, are you saying that we live within a multi-dimensional reality? Well, I don't know really. To be honest, it all looks just the same to me. In fact, if you hadn't mentioned it then I wouldn't have known that it was there at all. Life just seems to be all on the one level.

And we would agree. It is exactly because of this fundamental truth that it appears to be so, for we all live upon more than one plane of existence simultaneously and everything is integrated perfectly. It blends together seamlessly into the *singular* experience which we know of as our life. We have no need to think about it, for it just *is*. Indeed, truly has God thought. About everything.

Consider the cat and the dog. Do they think about their lives in the same way as does the human animal? Of course not, for they live instinctively knowing always what to do and when. They worry not and fear not. Truly do they live their lives unthinkingly on all levels at once, in the most natural way, and so do they live from moment to moment. They know who they are and live with joy.

If you watch very young children, then you will see that they have a similar approach to life and are fully focused within this moment. They are very aware of whatever they are doing and full of the fun and interest engendered therewith. They play like the cat and the dog and they do not work at life but just live it, joyfully.

And the energy flows, does it not? The natural exuberance and vitality of youth is truly a great *joy* to behold. Small children and animals express wonderfully that delightful miracle which is life. They live it and it *is*.

Whence then comes all of this energy and liveliness? An energy which often the adult can fail to keep up with, even though they are much bigger and stronger than the small child.

We would say to you that truly does the little child, which you see before you, consist of much more than the tiny body might at first suggest. Within the inner worlds that infant has access to resources undreamt of by the adult, who has become almost entirely focused upon the physical world and thus restricted in vision and awareness.

We might say that whereas the small child is focused only upon the experience of living, the adult has become much more attentive upon the everyday details of life. In so doing, have they moved their focus away from the inner worlds which as young children they lived so freely and so naturally.

Thus has the inborn wisdom of the child been lost, to the educated intellect and the narrowed understanding of the accepted truths of human society. Contact with the inner perspective has faded and no longer do they experience life with the fullness of their true being. That boundless vitality and spontaneous knowing of childhood has become but a dim memory, the vision lost within the timeless mists of the infinitely vast and endless oceans of eternal existence.

Like the outer physical dimension, the inner worlds have structure. This may be perceived using the psychic senses, which are a part of the etheric body. We might call this an *energy body*, for it is indeed the source of all the vitality which drives your earthly form.

When you let go of that bodily self, then quite simply do you just shut off the energy flow from your inner reality, your *etheric body.* A body which itself consists of an infinite number of other bodies, all of which connect to the multi-dimensional planes of existence within the inner world of the formless reality of nothing.

The mansions in God's House are infinite as are the rooms contained therein

Sensitivity

What does it mean to be sensitive? What is it to have sensitivity? The word sensitive comes from the Latin verb which means to feel. So, what does it mean to have feeling?

We might say that to feel is to experience the sense of touch. When we bang into something hard unexpectedly then we feel it, do we not? So to feel then is part of our physical reality and truly, do we experience that sense of touch most profoundly. We can say that we are all touched deeply, not just by the solid things but also by the events in our lives. For we can be sensitive to acts of kindness as well as those of harshness. Thus we feel on more than one level.

So our sensitivity is extant in both the physical and the non-physical realities of our life and this makes perfect sense, does it not? For if we could not *feel*, how could we live or experience anything at all? Must we not need to *feel* alive and be able to *feel* this life? Must we not be able to *feel* alive to the vibrant energies of the living world, which is all about us? We might say then that to feel is to have a sense of something. So are you *sensitive* to the life around you?

Can you feel it? Can you sense it? We do hope so, my friend. For if not, then indeed would you be dead to this world. You are a sentient conscious being and you are able to perceive the reality around you in which you have your being. You are connected. For truly, is life but the *one* experience, all contained within the loving embrace of the Divine Presence. Have you the ability to perceive this deep truth of your being, deep within your being? We would say yes, you do. For truly, do you have the sensitivity to *feel* and *know* Divine Love.

A sensitive then is someone who is very perceptive, able to sense and respond to the realities of different planes of existence. Able to perceive the many mansions in the Father's House and the infinite number of rooms contained therein. A sensitive is someone who has *awareness* of the formless reality of *nothing*.

As a very young child, we have access to these internal dimensions and so we instinctively live our lives and just simply *be* ourselves. Indeed, often we are not even aware of the fact that we are alive, for we just *are* and life just *is*.

But as we grow to adulthood, so do we begin to create complicated thought form structures within our minds which eventually obscure the inner worlds. We thus create mental filters and so in this way do we now become more fully focused upon this physical reality. This world which we have come here to experience and to live a full life upon this Earth. In truth, is all well. It is very well indeed.

This book is being written, *now*. It exists within this moment, *now*. For you to read, *now*. It has been created for people like yourself, who are becoming more aware *now* of those hidden realities which lie deep within. It is time *now* for you to bring your attention back once more to the inner realm and to focus afresh upon God's Truth.

To remember the reality of the Spirit within.

Many souls are now choosing to live a life upon Earth. Some would say that it is now becoming increasingly important that more people should have respect for Mother Nature, and indeed Mother Earth herself. They would say that it is becoming increasingly important for people to be more sensitive to the life which is all around them. To be aware of their actions and the consequences of those actions.

Whether your intellect believes it or not, Earth is indeed a sentient being. We shall be discussing the Earthly experience in Book Three of this series of books. But for now, let us accept the fact that there is a need to be more aware. A need to be more conscious. A need to be more *sensitive* to all of life, both seen and unseen.

May God's purpose be fulfilled in this world

Awareness

Let us consider once again the person who lives their life crossing over roads, without first looking out for any hazard. They are using free will to steer their ship of life and following in the wake of it will be their fate. Common sense does suggest, however, that they will not stay healthy for very long. But we also gave mention to a group of people who often do live long and may enjoy good health. People who might choose to live with expectation of health, wealth and happiness.

This group is smaller in number than you might think, for we speak not of money, power or material wealth. Instead, we talk of the few souls who are able to live a conscious life of spiritual awareness. An awareness which they could use to cross over any road and yet not come to any harm.

These are people who have walked their spiritual *path*. After many adventures requiring gallantry and courage, have they faced their fears and found the inner strengths of honesty and truth. With trust in themselves did they wend their way successfully forward to find that hidden *path*, which eventually would lead them on their Way towards the *Holy Mountain of Enlightenment*.

And then, with much effort and discipline did they find their Way up to the summit. They survived the stones and boulders which have fallen onto them and blocked the narrow Way. They have not lost their balance due to the winds of cause and effect, which blow very strongly at high altitude. Which might have caused them to fall from the *path* and to tumble down the steep mountainside back into the shadow of the low valley. A shadow which simply shows to them the direction to look, for the *Light*.

Finally, do they attain the summit and look up to that *Light*. They *feel* once more the warmth and comfort of the Divine Presence and they bask in the glory of the *Golden Light of Divine Love*.

That very same *Love* which has supported them and helped them along their *path*. Verily do we say unto thee, thou hast only to ask and help shall be given unto thee.

The spiritual disciple has to learn to ask for help, holding up their compass of *awareness* to the *light* will they be shown the Way. But first, must they find this inner compass within themselves. Like the piece of wood with two ends, the magnetic needle has two poles which are opposite yet are the same. The disciple must distinguish the two polarities and know North from South. Each is a relative polarity, depending upon where you are standing in the moment.

The most important lesson for any spiritual student is to learn to tell when a *truth* is before them. Learn to read the *signs* along the Way and distinguish the true directions from misleading ones. If you are travelling North and a sign says that you are going South then must it not be true unless, of course, you are mistaken in your sense of direction in which case you are indeed travelling South. To find the Way, the disciple needs always to make use of their inner compass.

So to find true North, must they learn to *sense* the polarity of the compass needle. To *feel* whether they are looking North or South as they perceive a possible truth. Developing their sensitivity, so that they feel with more clarity the direction in which their awareness is pointing. If they but hold up their inner compass to the *Light*, so shall they find illumination to see more clearly their spiritual *path*.

If they are successful in this endeavour and are able to reach the summit of the *Mountain*, then will they achieve knowing and thus experience awareness. They will know wholeness of being and they shall be arrayed in the armour of God and will know not fear but only the reflection of the *Light*.

With trust in our heart do we find awareness and see the light of divine love

PART V

THE END OF THIS BOOK

A Walk in the Park

One day, a man was walking across a city park. It was late in the morning and the weather had taken a turn for the worse. Freezing rain was lashing down and the poor man was absolutely soaked. He didn't have a raincoat and was feeling very miserable and cold, as he walked beneath a very large and ancient tree.

At that very moment the wind blew particularly hard. The old tree had finally had enough. It leaned over, suddenly cracking under the strain and many of its old roots snapped. With much creaking and groaning it fell over, right on top of the man. His injuries were so bad that he was in hospital for weeks and he sued the Council. He was successful and won a huge payout. The park manager, who had a young family, got the sack and lost his house.

The man had been late that day walking across the park because on the way into town he had got stuck in a traffic jam. He had caught the traffic because he had overslept that morning. The reason why he had overslept was because the day before he had worked late.

The reason why he had been working late that day was because the week before he had got angry and had a blazing row with his boss. As a result of this behaviour, his boss was now angry with him and had given him lots of extra work to do.

The beginning of this poor man's tribulations can be traced back to one particular morning, when he had got out of bed on the wrong side and stubbed his big toe painfully.

But, of course, it didn't really begin there...   because he had woken up with a bad hangover. He had got drunk the night before because he was alone and feeling very miserable. He had been so unhappy because that morning he had opened his bedroom curtains to find that the day was overcast, grey and miserable. Feeling down and depressed, he had looked forward to yet another gloomy day just like the one before.

One day, a man was walking across a city park. It was a beautiful sunny morning and he was thoroughly enjoying his day. A pleasant lady passed him by and he remarked how good the park was looking today. Responding with a big smile, she had agreed. He went on to say how the green was always in a perfect condition every day.

Now this lady happened to be the wife of the boss of the park manager. That evening, she told of her meeting with the man. Impressed, her husband had given a promotion to the park manager who was now able to move his young family out of their small cramped house and into a larger and more comfortable home.

The man had been enjoying his walk that morning because he was off work and so he had been able to avoid the traffic congestion on his way into town. He was feeling relaxed. The reason he had the day off was because he worked hard and had helped his boss the week before, who was so grateful that he had granted the man an extra day's holiday.

The start of this man's good fortune began one particular morning when he awoke early, drew back his bedroom curtains and saw the beginning of a bright new day. He had thanked God for giving him such a lovely day. Driving to work, he had thanked God again for giving him a wonderful job which he enjoyed so much.

But, of course, it didn't really begin there... the night before he had gone to a party. He had met many old friends and had enjoyed himself immensely. The morning before he had awoken late, opening his curtains upon a grey overcast day which looked dull and miserable. Smiling, he had thanked God for sending rain to all the plants. At that very moment, a gap appeared in the clouds and a bright beam of warm sunshine had shone down upon the man as he stood at the window.

Truly does the sun shine upon the joyous of heart

I Believe

So, my friend, what have you concluded so far? As we come to the end of this book, have you come to the end of your tether? Is your head so full of thoughts that you are no longer able to think clearly any more? Are you so bewildered, that you are now out of your mind? Maybe, you have lost your mind altogether!

What to believe or not to believe? Now that is the question! We would suggest that in human society people live within very complicated thought form structures, which have been created and built up over many generations.

In ages past, most humans lived in a world of superstitious or religious belief and today many people now live within a world of scientific belief. It matters not the label to which you attach that belief. With our thoughts do we make our reality. And so then what we think becomes our truth and it matters not whatever others may care to think about it.

But what exactly *is* a belief? We would say that it is simply a thought which you believe to be true. So, what do you believe? Have you found *your* truth yet? Have you found a truth in which you can believe, at last? We do hope so, my friend, because that has been our soul purpose in the writing of this book.

But what should we believe then, in this complicated world of today? Some scientists will announce one day that eating food is good for you and yet the very next day, another group are saying that eating food is bad for you.

Perhaps a particular religion might be telling you to do something in a certain way, whilst another will tell you to do something different. Sometimes, a culture may have a belief that to do something a certain way is lucky and brings good fortune. Whilst in a different culture, the very same superstition may be considered to be unlucky.

It is so difficult to know what to believe in these days, is it not? And we would agree. There is so much knowledge available today and much choice which has not been enjoyed by previous generations. We could say that life is no longer a simple affair for most people. So how then can we best decide as to what to believe or not to believe? How can we best decide as to what is true and what is not?

We might say that a belief is only a thought which you accept to be true. It is a thought which you have reflected within your own mind and then added to your mental thought structures. The question we would ask, however, is where did that thought first come from? Did it come from within yourself or without?

As a spiritual disciple will you need to learn to distinguish the difference between the two. Between inner and outer thought. And when you observe a truth within or without, then will you have need to make use of your inner compass in order to determine whether that truth is useful to you, or not.

As you walk lightly upon your *path* towards the *Mountain of Enlightenment*, so then shall you find that truths which are not so useful will lead you astray. They cause you to take a longer route to your goal. But sometimes the experience can be fun and may even prove to be worthwhile. For it is first necessary to *know* that which is not so useful, before you can *know* that which is useful.

Ultimately, will you begin to realise that each person lives their *own* truth. We each experience our individual reality of this world. And the pupil will begin to learn to rely much more upon the inner truths which are received from within. Truths which you *feel* within your heart. Truths which you *know* to be true. And if you know something then you have no need to believe it, for it *is* so.

Believe in yourself and let your heart show you the way

PART VI

CONTEMPLATIONS

Some Thoughts to Contemplate

This section of the book is designed for you to contemplate the mixed writings to be found herein. We would suggest that you focus upon one reading at a time, so that you may enter more fully the essence of the subject of the matter which is before you, that is to say, the words.

Perhaps you are new to meditation, my friend. If so, whenever you decide to meditate then try if you can to be sitting upright in a chair. This will help you to maintain a conscious focus, which in turn will help enhance the depth of your experience as you journey to the formless world of your inner realities.

In other words, sitting in a chair will help you to stay awake. It matters not, however, if you should seem to fall asleep. As you shall, in fact, be in an altered state of consciousness. Ask always to remember the detail of your journey before you begin. Then over time, as you more fully develop your skills in this discipline, will you learn to recall afterwards your experiences.

In addition, if you ask for understanding and knowing so also shall you begin to appreciate in more depth that experience, which will be deeper and more vivid if you are in a quiet place and without any disturbance. You will gradually learn to become more still as you relax. You may find also that you become very sensitive to noise and any loud sounds as you enter into the contemplation.

The more you practise this art, so will you begin to find yourself becoming very much more *aware* of everything that is around you. The quality of your journey will therefore depend entirely upon your strength of focus within. It is best then to be in as peaceful a state of *being* as possible.

Warning: Do not engage in any other kind of activity whilst you listen to the Audio Companion Collection of this book or while you are focused upon your meditations.

This Series has been especially designed for you to listen to an audio version, at the same time as you read parts III and IV of each book. Please visit *www.eternalspiritwithin.com* for details. You may find this experience to be extra-dimensional in nature.

For you will be involved in an exercise which uses and develops your psychic ability and thus shall you be in an altered state of consciousness. You will not be fully aware of this physical world about you.

But you do have free will, of course. You might decide to meditate whilst climbing the north face of the Eiger, or maybe while you are performing major brain surgery on a patient in an operating theatre. We would suggest, however, that neither the meditation nor the activity being undertaken will be at all successful.

The spiritual student will require wisdom in order to walk the *path*, lest they falter and fall even as they take their first steps upon their journey towards the *Mountain*. Take care therefore and think wisely as you live your life.

Remember that at all times are you responsible for your life. Truly, can you not blame another person or circumstance. Your thoughts, your decisions and your actions are yours and yours alone. For you are a creator and with *your* thoughts do you make *your* world.

May the love of God be with you, my friend

The White Telephone

You are sitting in an old and very comfortable armchair. Beside you is a lovely fire blazing away. You feel the gentle warmth on your legs, as you watch the lively flames dancing over the burning logs.

You hear the quiet crackle and pop of the fire as you sit back into the deep soft chair. You feel your feet placed firmly upon the floor. You lean back and relax more and more. The room is softly lit and very peaceful. Life is good. You feel calm. You feel still.

You take in a long slow breath, hold it for a moment and then breathe out gently. All of your worries and cares have now evaporated away into thin air and they are no more. You are relaxed and your body just seems to melt away to nothing, as you sit in the luxurious upholstery of the cosy old armchair. Everything feels good and you are feeling very relaxed.

As you are appreciating the warm glow of the fire, you begin to sense a subtle gentleness within the atmosphere of the room. You feel more and more relaxed. You turn to look away from the fire and near the chair you see a small polished table.

On this table is a white telephone. It is an old fashioned telephone with the metal dialling mechanism. You like its neat style and solid, chunky appearance.

It looks familiar to you, as you lean forwards to pick up the receiver. Holding it in your hand, you now place a finger into the round dial and begin to ring a number.

You let your finger pick the numbers for you.
Click wrrrrr, click wrrrrr, click wrrrr, click wrrrrr, click wrrrrr,

As you finish dialling, you lean back once more into the soft chair. You get yourself nice and comfortable again.

Holding the receiver to your ear, you hear the dialling tone as the phone rings at the other end of the line.
Burr burr, burr burr, burr burr, burr burr....

You are waiting for someone to pick up the other telephone.
You are relaxed. You are still. You are listening.

You hear a click on the line, as someone answers the phone....

.... you send them all your love, as the conversation now comes to an end. You place the receiver back down onto the telephone.

Leaning back once more, you feel the comfort of the old armchair. You are feeling very relaxed now as you feel a new joy within your heart. It's been so nice to hear their voice again and it's been lovely to be able to talk.

You look into the crackling flames and feel the warmth on your legs. The fire is beautiful. You are relaxed and feeling good. You move your hands. You move your feet. You open your eyes. You feel your feet placed firmly upon the floor. You are home. You are happy and so pleased that you have had contact again.

You breathe in slowly and close your eyes, as you remember the conversation which you have just had. It's been a lovely experience.

It was so good you have decided to call again soon.
You feel peaceful. You feel calm. You feel good and all is well.

The Castle of the Holy Grail

The energy which works the windlass,
to raise the drawbridge
into the Castle of the Grail,
is Pure Love.

The deep Moat surrounding the Castle
is full of fear, misgiving, doubt
and the darkness of sad emotion.

To find the Holy Grail and
complete the Quest,

To finally enter the Narrow Way,
you need to find pure Divine Love
within yourself.

You then become as One
with the windlass,
and so able to lower
the drawbridge yourself.

No one else can do it for you.
You will stand and wait for all Eternity
even after all the toil to find the Castle,
if you make no effort to love purely.

God is Love

God is Love, Love is God.
God is in all things, Love is in all things.
Love is at the heart of all things, yet we see it not.

We appear to see that which is the opposite of love. We see
violence, hatred and deceit. We see people hurting each other.
But this is an illusion, however, for in reality there is no opposite
to love. For love just is.

We are seeing people in pain, turmoil and distress. And in that
distress they hit out at others and cause pain. You see not hatred,
but anguish. Compassion and not judgement is called for.
To respond with compassion is an act of love.

Although invisible, this love can be felt by us. We recognise an act
of love not by the action itself, but by the feeling which it fosters
within us.

We feel the reaction within our hearts and though we see it not, yet
can we feel it. Perhaps we could describe it as a *presence*, for it has
existence but no apparent form.

God exists, yet we see God not. Love exists, yet we see Love not.
Love is an energy. We feel it's presence eternally, yet we see it not.

Compassion is an act of love. And in that moment do you not feel
a giving out from your heart? Love is an act of giving.

God gives us life. And is this not an act of love?
Deep within, our soul energy is *one* with God.
Our soul is the expression of Love.
Love is the expression of our soul.

To Know Love

To know Love
we must reach through the pain
and touch
the joy in God's heart.

To know illumination
we must not turn away from a lesson of pain
but accept it for otherwise
we shall not be strong enough of heart
to face the truth
which gives us illumination.

To know Light
we must face the darkness
and see through it to the Light hidden within
waiting to be seen.

You Are

Have patience my friend, know that all is well.
Have trust my friend, trust in your life
And let not your heart be troubled.

As you choose to focus upon the disharmony about you
Then your consciousness, indeed your very being,
Becomes that upon which you are looking.

Almighty God, the Divine Spirit says
I am that which I am.
We would say to you
That you are that which you are.

If you look at sadness, will you become sad.
If you look at violence, will you become violent.
If you look at anger, will you become angry.

If you are still, then you become that stillness.
If you are content, then you become that contentedness.
If you are thoughtful, then you become those thoughts.
So learn to take care, as you look at your world about you.

We wish to say to you
That the great truths of this universe
Are truly very simple,
Only the Fool has the wisdom to see it.

And this truth is joy,
And this truth is abundance,
And this truth is love.

Look to the Joyful and you will become Joy.
Look to the Abundance and you will become Abundant.
Look to the Love and you will become Love.
God bless you and peace be with you.

To Find Love

First find and identify that pure selfless divine love within yourself, it is buried beneath the pain.

Then gradually by effort combine with it, so that by degrees you are able to manifest and to express that love to everything around you.

When you eventually can express the pure love within you to all life around you at all times, then will you have become that Love.

You will have found
Peace.
You will have found
God.

For God *is*
that Divine Love
which you are expressing.

Feel The Spirit

Feel the Love
Feel the Light
Feel the Spirit
As you allow yourself to feel joy
So then will you free yourself from bondage.

You know this
So simply allow joy to be
Allow yourself to be.

The joy in your heart will lift you up
Into the Realms of Glory and you will know
Indeed you already know all that you need to know.

So just be
It is now the time for you to just be
Allow yourself to relax into the love and joy
The peace and stillness which has always been yours.

Allow it all to be
Believe in yourself
Believe in who you are.

I Am That I Am

I am that I am
I make the wind move across the waters
I move the Sun across the sky.

I spin the Earth to give you day and night
The stars are mine, I have created them
The Universe is mine, I have created it.

Infinite Universes have I created
Each unique and individual
As are you my Children.

My Universes are vast to your reality
Yet you are each an Individual Universe, with galaxies of stars.

You consist of trillions of atoms
Billions of molecules
Millions of cells
Each a unique and individual tiny speck of light.

My Light
Tiny specks of light which are as the multitude of stars in your sky
You each sparkle to me in your Glory.

You each are a radiant being of Light
Sparks of the Divine
See yourselves as you truly are
My Children of Light.

So does my Light shine from your hearts
I am in all things
That which you see, I am
That which you see not, I am.

Light of the Sun
I am
Light of your hearts
I am
Light of your thoughts
I am
Light of your being
I am.

I am vast
I am all that is
I am now.

I am time
I am the space between time
I am movement and I am stillness.

I am you
You are eternal
Know this to be so
And
Let your Light
Shine out into the Universe.

I Am, Within and Without

I am within yet I am without, for I am in all things. Love me within and love me without, for my love is in all things. When you do not feel my love, you are unhappy for you are alone. You are feeling no contact with me.

To find your contact, your touch with me, then love within and love without. My love touches *all* and connects *all*. There is no separation within my love, only without my love.

My love is warm. My love is light. My love is life. To know life then you must know my love. To know my love then you must know my light.

Follow my light to find my guidance. Follow my guidance to find my illumination. Follow my illumination to find my Love. Follow my Love to find my Life. For *I am* The Way. You cannot find me through another. You must come to me alone and in the wilderness will I feed you and clothe you with Gold.

Conclusion

The big jumbled jumble of all my belongings which have gradually accumulated slowly over the years, finally got sorted out. I cleared my space and I cleared my mind. Then at last, I sat down to write. I was most surprised to find, however, that I had already written the beginning of the book eleven months previously!

No, this was not the start or the beginning but that other beginning in Part III, where my friends in spirit had started to communicate and to write this book with me. Thereafter the urgent need to write was a constant presence, until finally the pressure became too much and I just *had* to sit down and put pen to paper.

To my great delight the paragraphs began to appear one after the other. As I sat at the computer typing up my notes the words seemed to take shape upon the screen in front of me, very much as if I was creating a piece of sculpture. I felt such a great joy as each page was finished.

The actual manuscript was written in only 54 days but the physical creation of the book itself took much longer. As I worked with it, sometimes I awoke with a sentence in my head which I then needed to insert somewhere within the text. At other times, I just had to keep going back to a page and read it over and over again. Eventually I spotted the error or made the small changes which were required.

This book has definitely not been created in any intellectual sense, for at no time has it been planned out or thought through. It all just happened somehow and everything fell into place perfectly. As I started each subject, one after the other, all I had was the title and a blank sheet! It was wonderful to watch as each page took shape and most of the time I hadn't a clue as to how they were going to finish it! So this then was the manner in which the book gradually began to take form. Each paragraph was a piece of the jigsaw puzzle and they were given to me in perfect order one by one. All I had to do was to assemble the picture in front of me.

This book is really two books in one for it is a spoken text as well as it is a written one and so this makes punctuation a big problem because if I edited the book too heavily then the flow of the energy contained within the words is lost and so then has the purpose of the book itself also been lost. There are many layers of deep meaning hidden within this volume and it truly is multi-dimensional in nature. I hope that you have enjoyed reading it as much as I have enjoyed myself in the writing of it.

I would like to thank all my friends who have helped me along the Way. I especially wish to thank Joanne for allowing my friends in spirit to speak to me that day in the kitchen, when they were trying to encourage me to start this book and for the lovely gift of bringing through the picture for the front cover. A big thank you also to Vanessa who helped me to keep going during the writing of the manuscript. It was her guide who told me that I was writing a trilogy and not just the one book! Thanks go to Juls for all her help, too. I also wish to thank Niki for reading the text through carefully and allowing my editors-in-spirit to highlight small details which were needing attention.

Although I was already aware of the knowledge which is contained within this book, the manner in which it has been expressed is certainly not mine. I have not only gained a much deeper understanding of it but I have also *lived* it and that was a very intense experience indeed, believe me! It's been wonderful to see how all of these ideas have been carefully put together, rather like the patchwork of an embroidered quilt. You may find that the patterns which you observe in this quilt will vary according to how you are looking at it.

They do say, don't they, that we can experience a second childhood as we get older. I remember when, as a child, I seemed to lose my sense of inner peace. I was blissfully unaware that it even existed until I had lost it and in the course of writing this book I have found it once again. In a sense, I have become like the child I once was. I am now more fully aware and conscious of that peace, which I had once taken for granted as a natural part of my being.

Isn't it a strange thing to think of how all the billions of individuals alive on Earth, at this very moment, are each living their *own* truths. Each person has a unique perspective, with their own personal take on things. So perhaps we really are all here just for the ride, for the fun of the fair....

I know that *truth* is contained within these pages. It is the eternal truth of the Spirit within. A truth which has been expressed down the Ages by countless teachers, throughout human history. It is a truth which will continue to express itself through many more teachers, in times to come. I sincerely hope that you have recognised and remembered a little more of your own truth, as I have mine.

I wish you all the best, as you continue your voyages of life across the infinitely vast and endless oceans of eternal existence. Remember to appreciate the warmer and more tranquil waters and to steam head on into the storms, if you find that you cannot steer around them.

Full Steam Ahead!
Bon Voyage....

We do so hope that you have enjoyed
our short dissertation, my friend.
May peace be with you.

Amen

Afterword

Although I had spiritual knowledge
I had not my truth

In the writing of this book for you
I have found that truth

I am a writer
I bless you and thank you
because without you
I would not at last be feeling
my joy

A joy that is ultimately
my truth

I pray that joy becomes
your truth

Amen

Barry Robinson
www.eternalspiritwithin.com

Lightning Source UK Ltd.
Milton Keynes UK
UKOW06f0512030216

267652UK00002B/96/P